FROM PEEP SHOW TO PALACE

LIMBS AND LENSES

A gathering of London gaiety girls invade wizard Edison's laboratory at Orange, N. J., and give an exposition of their dances before the Kinetoscope.

FROM PEEP SHOW TO PALACE

The Birth of American Film

David Robinson

FOREWORD BY MARTIN SCORSESE

NEW YORK

COLUMBIA UNIVERSITY PRESS

in association with the Library of Congress, Washington, D.C.

Columbia University Press thanks the Madison Council, the private sector advisory group to the Library of Congress, for their generous contribution toward the cost of publishing this book.

Columbia University Press
New York   Chichester, West Sussex
Foreword © 1996 Martin Scorsese
Captions and index © 1996 Columbia University Press

Library of Congress Cataloging-in-Publication Data

Robinson, David. 1930–
     From peep show to palace : the birth of American film / David
Robinson ; foreword by Martin Scorsese.
        p.   cm.
     Includes bibliographical references and index.
     ISBN 0-231-10338-7 (alk. paper)   PA ISBN 0-231-10339-5
     1. Motion pictures—United States—History.   2. Motion picture
industry—United States—History.   I. Title.
PN1993.5.U6R59   1995
791.43'0973—dc20   95-19014
                                                              CIP

p 10 9 8 7 6 5 4 3 2 1

FRONTISPIECE: "Limbs and Lenses," *National Police Gazette*, November 24, 1894.

CONTENTS

❶

PIECES IN A PUZZLE
Prehistory of the motion picture   2

❷

SORCERER AND APPRENTICE
Edison, Dickson, and the Kinetoscope   18

❸

FROM SCIENCE TO SHOW BUSINESS
Development of the Kinetoscope, as medium and commerce   36

⓫

FEATURES AND PALACES
Revolutions in exhibition

⓬

THE YEAR 1913
The cinema comes of age

INTRODUCTION

James H. Billington
The Librarian of Congress

The Library of Congress has been actively involved in the history of cinema since October 6, 1893, when W. K. L. Dickson, assistant to Thomas Edison and inventor of the Kinetoscope, recorded the first copyright registration for a commercially distributed movie. Dickson's claim marked the beginning of the film industry in America and it predated by more than two years the Lumière brothers projection of a film before a paying audience in Paris on December 28, 1895, the date generally accepted for the invention of the cinema. Ever since Dickson's historic copyright claim, the Library has maintained records on every film copyrighted in America.

Today, the Library of Congress makes accessible to scholars and researchers the largest collection of films in the world. The Library leads the film archive movement in the United States and, since 1969, has undertaken more than half of all the 35mm film preservation completed in the United States.

In 1993, we completed *A Study of the Current State of American Film Preservation*; in 1994, we published *Redefining Film Preservation: A National Plan*, based on the study's findings. These assessments, which were written in cooperation with the film industry, the film archives, and the academic community, should significantly improve the quantity and quality of film preservation undertaken in this country.

This volume was generously funded by the Library's James Madison Council, its private sector advisory group, in recognition of our continuing role as a leading world institution in both film preservation and cinema research.

The Library of Congress was involved with the infant movie industry from its beginning. In August 1893, W. K. L. Dickson sent the Library's Copyright Office an application to register a motion picture with the enigmatic title *Edison Kinetoscopic Records*. The work was officially accepted on October 6, 1893, when this registration was recorded and signed by the Librarian of Congress, A. R. Spofford. The two-month delay may have been caused by questions to Dickson about the nature of the material and decisions as to whether Kinetoscopic records were something that could be registered under existing copyright laws. Dickson had been registering photographs for several years and he submitted this and subsequent motion picture registrations under the regulations for registering still photographs and the Copyright Office accepted them as photographs. It was a fortunate decision because Dickson's practice was adopted by subsequent motion picture producers who registered and deposited several thousand of the industry's first productions at the Library of Congress. Between 1894 and 1913, more than 3,000 nearly complete motion pictures and fragments of several thousand others were added to the Library's collections. With the passage of a century, time and chemistry destroyed many of the originals, but almost all of the copies at the Library of Congress survived to become a treasured record of the beginning of the movies.

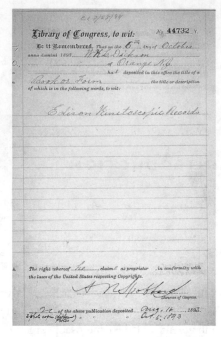

The early silent period is the least known area of cinema history and the Library's collection is particularly rich in films produced before 1915. Mr. Robinson tells with verve the fascinating story of the transition from pre-cinematic forms before 1893 to the major world industry that motion pictures became within the next two decades.

During its first century, the cinema has been remarkable in its artistic achievement and in what it has accomplished as a medium of communication between the peoples of the world. We expect that the next hundred years of movie history will be no less fruitful.

INTRODUCTION

FOREWORD

Martin Scorsese

THERE HAS ALWAYS BEEN A MAGIC TO THE MOVIES. WE ALL
know, of course, that movies are the product of science and technology. But
an aura of magic has enveloped them right from the beginning. The men who
invented movies—Edison, Lumière, and Méliès—were scientists with the
spirit of showmen: rather than simply analyze motion, they transferred it into
a spectacle. In their own way, they were visionaries who attempted to convert
science into a magical form of entertainment.

David Robinson, a historian and a film critic for the London *Times*, has
written a fascinating history of the first twenty years of American cinema,
from Edison's peep-show Kinetoscope in 1893 to the construction of the first
movie palace in 1913. Robinson doesn't simply rely on what earlier scholars
have written about the period—rather he carefully studied the original Edison papers, early motion picture trade journals, and legal documents that
were used in early patent litigation. By doing so, he gives us an archeology of
early motion picture showmanship as he traces the origins of film back to
lantern slide shows.

Robinson's book brought to mind one of my primal film experiences, *The
Magic Box*, a 1951 British film directed by John Boulting—as far as I know,
the only film ever made about the invention of cinema. I was ten years old
when my father took me to see it. The film told the story of the British inventor, William Friese-Greene, one of the unsung pioneers of the invention of
cinema.

There's a scene in which Friese-Greene explains the concept of motion
pictures to his girlfriend by flipping a series of drawings he's made on the

margins of a book: these are all separate, static images, but when they're flipped, they miraculously *move*. For the first time I understood what motion pictures were and I haven't been the same since. But this film also showed the life of Friese-Greene, and watching the spectacle of this man suffering to create an incredible machine that would open the horizons of the human mind and soul left an indelible mark on me.

I think about that film constantly. What did I find so astonishing about it? The beautiful color? The style? The struggle to perfect the technology that made movies? The human story of Friese-Greene, his family's struggle? Perhaps it was all these elements, because together they form Friese-Greene's obsession that I share and that I carry with me to this day. The same wonder I experienced watching the persistence of vision sequence in *The Magic Box* I still experience today in the presence of editing, where another kind of magic takes place. You take two pieces of film. One piece moves and the other piece moves, and when you cut them together, the connection forms a new movement in the mind's eye—but it's a collective as well as an individual mind. This new movement is truly the *language* of cinema. Ultimately the audience shares this experience, this emotion, this memory, through this new language. It's no wonder that Friese-Greene was so driven, just as I'm sure Edison, Lumière, and Méliès were: they were in awe of their own creation. They had found the key to another level of human experience.

Today, we take the machinery of the cinema for granted, and with a few exceptions most of the cinema's pioneers are long forgotten. But the magic that they worked still holds us in its thrall. This book pays tribute to these scientists and visionaries. Their work captured the imagination of the world, and permanently transformed our culture. For the past one hundred years, we have all been the children of their cinema.

PREFACE AND ACKNOWLEDGMENTS

THE EVOLUTION OF THE MOTION PICTURE WAS A LENGTHY and tortuous process, and the progression of the first years of the cinema was no less complex, involving the exploration of a technology, the discovery of an art, the creation of an industry, the conquest of an audience.

This book is an attempt to trace as clear and direct a path as possible through the entanglements of the story, for the sake of readers curious to discover the main contours of the prehistory and early history of our century's most potent medium of communication.

The story begins with the archeological age, the exploration of those disparate elements—projection, photography, the analysis and synthesis of motion—which ultimately came together in the motion picture film as we know it today. From the moment of the arrival of the cinema we are concerned with the parallel development of technique, art, spectacle, and industry.

The choice of the year 1913 to end this brief record is not arbitrary, nor made simply because it closes a neat two-decade period from the perfecting of the Kinetoscope. By chance, a period of a bare twelve months saw the coincidental consolidation of a whole complex of developments, to make this year a watershed in the history of cinema. The period before 1913 was a time of experiment and evolution; when that year ended—the last, as it happened, of the old world that vanished with the First World War—the future structures of the industry, particularly in the United States, were definitively formed.

The short bibliography at the end acknowledges works that have been consulted for the purposes of this little work, and suggests sources for further reading. I must acknowledge a continuing debt to those pioneer historians like Henry V. Hopwood, Terry Ramsaye, Benjamin Hampton, and Georges Sadoul who were in time to save much evidence before it was lost, and whose work has not lost its value. The key source for the Edison–Dickson story remains the exemplary researches of the late Gordon Hendricks, even if some of his conclusions now seem a trifle impetuous. Among the indispensable contemporary historians are John Barnes, Laurent Mannoni, Brian Coe, Hermann Hecht, and the authors of the current *History of the American Cinema:* I have inevitably made use of the incomparably researched volumes by Charles Musser and Eileen Bowser.

Most of all though I have treasured those invaluable witnesses who, uninhibited by any regard for posterity or historical self-importance, contributed a continuing, intelligent, enthusiastic critical commentary on the cinema of their times in the pages of The Moving Picture World, The New York Dramatic Mirror, The Kinematograph Weekly, The Bioscope, and the other trade papers of the day.

Finally, special thanks are due to the staffs of the Edison Historic Site in West Orange, New Jersey, and of the Motion Picture, Broadcasting, and Recorded Sound Division of the Library of Congress, who initiated this project. Particular gratitude is due to its chief, David Francis, to Pat Loughney, to Pat Sheehan, to Madeline Matz, to Ken Weissman, and to Paul Spehr, who was companion and counselor on explorations of treasure houses like the Edison Site and the U.S. Patent Office, where he shared the once-in-a-lifetime thrill of opening up a document to reveal a long-forgotten fragment of the first Kinetoscope film, and who prepared the photo captions, the photo credits, and the index. Finally, I would like to pay special tribute to Sarah Rouse, who undertook the onerous task of reading all the proofs.

FROM PEEP SHOW TO PALACE

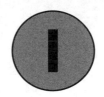

PIECES IN A PUZZLE

Prehistory of the motion picture

THE MOTION PICTURE AS WE KNOW IT WAS NEVER IN THE strict sense "invented." Nor was its development even a normal process of evolution. Rather it was like the assembling of a puzzle, the pieces of which were only vouchsafed intermittently, over a very long period of time. The puzzle pieces were the several elements that had eventually to be combined to perfect a device to produce and project animated photographs.

The most apparent antecedent of the cinema projector is the magic lantern. As early as 1420 Giovanni da Fontana, a young Venetian academic in Padua, proposed the mischievous notion of painting demonic shapes on the horn window of an ordinary lantern in order to frighten people with the grotesque shadows thereby cast upon a wall. Without a condenser to concentrate the lamplight or a lens to focus the image, however, Giovanni's shadows must have been fairly vague; almost two and a half centuries more passed before the lantern acquired the magic of precise representation.*

---

*Discussion of the magic lantern presents a problem of nomenclature. For the first two centuries of its life the name "magic lantern," with its various literal translations, was universal. In America, however, the term "stereopticon" became increasingly current after the 1850s. This essential misnomer seems to have originated with the first photographic lantern slides marketed by the Langenheim brothers, which were often made from one half of a stereoscopic double negative.

In the nineties the word had a brief vogue in Britain; the *Optical and Magic Lantern Journal* noted: "The word stereopticon, which is in general use in America, is becoming more and more used in this country. When talking to a stereopticon operator lately, he gave it as his experience that people would more readily attend a lecture which was to be

In 1645 the polymath Jesuit scholar Athanasius Kircher (1602–1680) described and illustrated a device for reflecting the light of the sun from a mirror, through a lens, and on to a screen. If some message were written in inverted opaque letters on the mirror, this would appear in the light on the screen. Kircher showed that a similar effect could be obtained at night by the use of a candle and a water-filled spherical glass to condense its light. Only a slight readjustment of these elements—light source, condenser, image painted on glass, lens—was necessary to arrive at the magic lantern.

In 1671, in a new edition of his book *Ars Magna Lucis et Umbrae* (*The Great Art of Light and Shadow*), Kircher himself described and illustrated magic lanterns—unfortunately rather inaccurately. Since these were the very first printed illustrations of the magic lantern, Kircher has frequently been credited with its invention, but a more likely claimant appears to be the Dutch physicist Christiaan Huygens, whose correspondence shows him to have been using a practical magic lantern as early as 1659. Huygens dealt with a London optician named Richard Reeves, who was selling lanterns by 1663 (Samuel Pepys bought one on August 19, 1666, two weeks before the Great Fire of London). Several years before Kircher's description, too, a Danish scientist, Thomas Rasmussen Walgenstein—the first writer to use the name Laterna Magica—was demonstrating the device in various European cities.

Throughout the next century the magic lantern had a double life. In the cabinets of physicists and gentlemen of a scientific bent it was an optical curiosity of no particular utility. At the other end of the social scale it was taken up by itinerant entertainers who traveled Europe giving shows in genteel drawing rooms, if they were lucky, or more often in barns and inns where they delighted rustic audiences with a mixture of fright and fun.

Until the end of the eighteenth century, however, the scope of the lantern was restricted by the weak illumination supplied by animal and vegetable oil. In the 1780s a Swiss scientist, Ami Argand, devised and patented an improved lamp that provided a light source strong enough to make the lantern capable

---

illustrated with stereopticon views than one illustrated with lantern views. The name, he says, has something mysterious about it as yet, and many people think it has to do with some new invention. Anyhow, he explained, by adopting this name, we get a larger audience than we would with the usual name." After 1880 the term "optical lantern" was introduced in Britain by J. F. Dallmeyer in an endeavor to eradicate the pleasantly irrational suggestions of the old term.

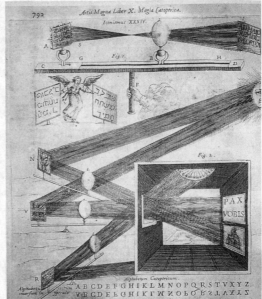

A crude antecedent of the modern projector was portrayed by Giovanni da Fontana in 1420 (above left). In the seventeenth century, more practical projectors began to appear. Athanasius Kircher illustrated the use of mirrors to reflect an illuminated image in the 1645 edition of *Ars Magna Lucis et Umbrae* (above right) and an almost workable magic lantern in the 1671 edition (right).

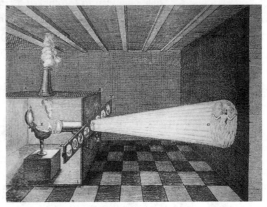

of theatrical exhibition. The first notable showman to take advantage of this new technology was the Belgian-born Etienne Gaspard Robertson. Recognizing the appetite of the late eighteenth-century public for Gothic horror, he devised a show which he called the Phantasmagoria. His theater was a former Capuchin chapel in revolutionary Paris, where he thrilled his audience with visions of ghosts and demons, projected from behind a translucent screen. Ghostly effects were obtained by projecting onto smoke, while his most notable invention was the Phantascope, a special lantern that was moved toward or away from the screen, the focus being constantly adjusted, so that images

■   In Paris, during the French Revolution, Etienne Gaspard Robertson employed a magic lantern to astound and frighten audiences in his *Phantasmagoria*. Images of ghosts and demons materialized on walls or on clouds of smoke, appearing to grow and shrink with dramatic abruptness.

appeared to grow or shrink dramatically. Robertson's own son Eugene was one of several European showmen who introduced Phantasmagoria shows to the New World.

Further technical advances like the invention of the brilliant limelight encouraged new elaborations in lantern shows. In the 1830s "dissolvent" or "dissolving" views explored a whole range of effects achieved by mixing or superimposing the images projected by two (and later three or even, exceptionally, four) lantern objectives. The pioneer and greatest exponent of dissolving view painting was Henry Langdon Childe (1781–1874), who in his eighties was still creating spectacular lantern shows for the Royal Polytechnic, a famous institution of Victorian London, set up for the dissemination of popular science and exhibition of new inventions.

By the late nineteenth century, in fact, the ambitions of the magic lantern clearly anticipated the cinema. The lantern was used to create narrative and spectacle; and from an early stage there was a dominant desire to make the screen image move. By pulling a long slide through the gate of the lantern, the seventeenth-century lanternists caused a procession of figures to pass across the screen. As early as 1736 a Dutch mathematician, Pieter van Muss-

■ During the nineteenth century showmen used colorfully painted glass slides to create intricate, elaborate magic lantern shows that anticipated cinema. Lanterns equipped with several lenses dissolved from one visual effect to another, telling stories, illustrating songs, or exploring foreign lands. A hand-painted slide, made about 1800, depicts the Sun King, Louis XIV of France.

chenbroek, published details of a series of mechanical slides he had devised. His technique of painting images on two layers of glass which could be moved independently by means of levers, slides, or ratchets so as to produce change or motion in the screen image, continued to be employed, with ever-increasing variety and sophistication, throughout the whole career of the magic lantern. Indeed, as Brian Coe writes, "by the time that the first movie films appeared at the end of the last century, the magic lantern was capable of very advanced, beautiful, even realistic effects. For some of those who saw the early films, with their jumpy, dim, black and white images, they seemed no advance at all."

Movement in the lantern image was produced by mechanical devices. The essential difference in the cinema is that the illusion of movement is achieved by exploiting a curious physiological phenomenon popularly known as "the persistence of vision." The simplest illustration of this principle, observed since ancient times, is the effect produced when a burning brand is rapidly rotated in the dark, producing the illusion of a continuous circle of light. One of several scholars to be intrigued by such optical effects, Peter Mark Roget (subsequently compiler of the celebrated *Thesaurus*) read a paper to the Royal Society of London in December 1824, analyzing the curious illusions afforded when moving spoked wheels are viewed through the intervals of a series of vertical bars. The illusions were produced, he realized, by the phenomenon that a visual impression persists in the brain for a brief but determinate interval after the object which made that impression has been withdrawn, or has changed its place.

Other scientists explored the idea. Sir John Herschel is said to have demonstrated the principle by the simple trick of spinning a shilling and showing that both sides of the coin are visible simultaneously, apparently superimposed. In 1826 John Ayrton Paris published a scientific toy called the thaumatrope. This consisted of a disk of cardboard with the separate parts of one picture printed on each of its two sides. When the disk was rapidly revolved by means of threads attached at its sides, the two sides of the disk appeared to merge as one picture.

On December 10, 1830, the eminent physicist Michael Faraday read a paper to the Royal Institution, "On a Peculiar Class of Optical Deception." Inspired by his observation of toothed mill wheels, he created a device by which two toothed wheels were rotated on the same axis but in opposite directions. By adjusting the relative speed and observing one of the wheels through the teeth of the other, the viewer received the impression that the observed wheel was standing still or moving very slowly in one direction or another. The phenomenon could be displayed even more simply if the reflection of a disk revolved before a mirror were observed through slots at equal intervals around its circumference.

This effect was produced because each slot in the near wheel afforded so brief a glimpse of the other that it appeared to be stationary. After this glimpse the vision was obstructed by the solid part of the front wheel until the next slot and the next brief and seemingly stationary glimpse. Because of the phenomenon of the persistence of vision, the eye and the brain put together this series of glimpses to give the impression of a continuous view of a stationary wheel.

Roget's paper also inspired a Belgian physicist and artist, Joseph Antoine Ferdinand Plateau, to make his own studies. Plateau developed Faraday's wheel into a delightful optical toy. Around the edge of the disk, between the slots, he placed a series of drawings of a figure in successive phases of some action. When the disk was viewed in a mirror, through the slots, the figure appeared stationary, but the phases of its action were all joined together, giving an impression of motion. The first cartoon figure—it was in fact a little dancer—was brought to life. Plateau called his toy the Phenakistiscope, from Greek words meaning "deceiver" and "to see"; though when it was marketed in England by the publisher Rudolph Ackermann, the name was changed to Phantasmascope and subsequently to Fantascope.

It seemed characteristic of the process of scientific discovery that led to the cinema that at a certain moment an idea was in the air, almost mystically striking different people in different places at the same time. Roget later

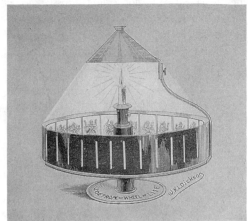

■ Persistence of vision is illustrated by two other popular nineteenth-century amusements. The images painted around the outside of the Phenakistiscope disk (left) appear as a single moving image when the spinning disc is watched in a mirror through the slots. In the Zoetrope (right), illustrated strips of paper are placed inside of a drum and viewed through slits in the side as it revolves. Zoetrope strips can be changed and several viewers can watch at the same time. The drawing of the Zoetrope was made by movie pioneer W. K. L. Dickson.

claimed, without resentment, that he had himself made several Phenakistiscopes in the spring of 1831. Platcau's device was published early in 1833, and almost simultaneously but independently Simon Stampfer of Vienna produced a nearly similar toy which he called the Stroboscope.

The following year William George Horner proposed a more convenient device that did away with the need for a mirror and permitted several viewers to watch the illusion at the same time. Horner's Daedalum took the form of an open-topped drum with slots around the side. The picture series, on long strips of paper rather than disks, were placed around the inside of the drum, and viewed through the slits as it revolved. Strangely the device was not commercially developed for more than thirty years, until 1867, when it was patented almost simultaneously in England by M. Bradley and in America by William F. Lincoln, who gave it the name of Zoetrope.

The attempt to link these moving picture devices to the magic lantern was inevitable. The earliest recorded projecting apparatus to use the persistence of

■ In 1843, T. W. Naylor proposed projecting moving images from painted glass disks similar to the Phenakistiscope (above right). Ross' *Wheel of Life,* patented in England in 1871, used a revolving shutter to improve the quality of projected movement (below right). The shutter replaced the slots in the Phenakistoscope.

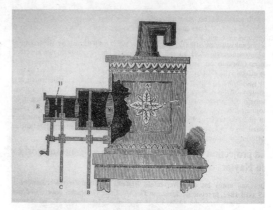

vision principle was described by T. W. Naylor of Newcastle-upon-Tyne in 1843. Naylor proposed painting the images of a phenakistiscope around the perimeter of a glass disk, which was then revolved between the condenser and lens of a magic lantern. A second, opaque disk, pierced with apertures corresponding to the images, was revolved at the same speed and on the same axle in front of the lens. Naylor's apparatus undoubtedly worked, though the shutter would have severely restricted the light, and the images must have been somewhat blurred.

Naylor's plan was however published in several German scientific papers and, in 1845 an Austrian officer, Franz von Uchatius, took up the idea to create his own projecting version of Stampfer's Stroboscope. A disk with 12 transparent series drawings around its edge revolved in front of the projection beam, while a second disk pierced with 12 apertures revolved, unlike Naylor's, in the opposite direction. The disadvantage of this method was again the degree of light cut out by the shutter disk. A quarter of a century later, in 1871, T. Ross of England patented his perfected version of a smaller, commercial version of Uchatius' device. In this a single-slot shutter revolved thirteen times for every revolution of the thirteen-phase images of the picture disk.

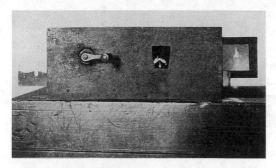

■ The Choreutoscope, developed by J. S. Beale in 1866 (left), paired a shutter with a "Geneva stop mechanism" (sometimes called a "Maltese cross") to create the rapid succession of separate images indispensable for an illusion of motion—a combination used in many motion picture cameras and projectors. In 1877, Emile Reynaud patented the Praxinoscope (below left), an improvement to the Zoetrope. Instead of viewing through slots, strips of images placed in the drum could be viewed in a prism of mirrors mounted at the center of the drum.

The central challenge in all these persistence of vision devices—the same problem that would tax the pioneers of motion pictures—was to present to the eye a rapid succession of apparently stationary images. This could be achieved by one of two basic methods, which were to compete in the various experiments that paved the way to the cinema. In most of the earlier moving image machines, the images passed before the eye in continuous, uninterrupted motion, while some form of shutter or interrupted illumination permitted only a brief, flash perception of each separate image as it passed.

The alternative was some mechanism that would give an intermittent motion to the images—stopping each one for a brief fraction of a second, and then substituting the next, while in some way concealing from the eye the intermediate movement from one still image to another. This was the solution adopted by J. S. Beale in his Choreutoscope (1866), an elaborate form of lantern slide. Six progressive images were painted on a strip of glass, which was intermittently moved and stopped, to present each image in turn before the lens aperture. The aperture was covered by a shutter during the intervals of movement. The intermittent movement was achieved by the use of the Geneva stop mechanism, which, as the "Maltese cross," would become an important element in the development of film cameras and projectors.

Animated drawings produced by means of persistence of vision reached their zenith in the work of the Frenchman Emile Reynaud. In 1877 Reynaud patented his Praxinoscope. This was essentially a revolving drum like the zoetrope, but instead of being viewed through slots, the images were seen reflected in a prism of mirrors at the center of the drum. Each mirror as it passed flashed a clear, stationary impression of the image opposed to it. The result was perfect animation, with no loss of light. Reynaud went on to make a Praxinoscope Theater, in which the moving figure was superimposed upon a reflected decor. His next development was a projecting Praxinoscope, in which the lantern beam shone through transparent images as they revolved on a drum, and was thence reflected by a mirror-prism and projected through the lens—a remarkable recapitulation of Kircher's mirror projection of 1646.

In 1892 Reynaud developed this idea into a theatrical entertainment, the Théatre Optique. Until this time the movement in all persistence of vision animation devices had been limited to the repetitive cyclic form of images around a disk or cylinder. Reynaud now had the idea of painting series of pictures on small glass plates, which were joined together in a flexible strip whose length was limited only by the size of the drums between which it was wound. In this way Reynaud was able to use his animated characters to perform mime plays as long as ten minutes or more. The playlets were projected from behind the screen, superimposed on decors projected from a second lantern. The Théatre Optique came remarkably close to the cinema. All that was missing was photography.

From 1852 (the date of a patent by Jules Dubosq of Paris) onward, there were suggestions for using photographic images in Phenakistiscopes and Zoetropes; and in 1870 Henry R. Heyl succeeded in giving an impression of motion to a series of projected photographs of a couple waltzing. The drawback with all these devices was that every single photographic image had to be made separately. Exposure times were slow and the most sensitive medium, wet collodion, required each plate to be prepared immediately before the photograph was made. Heyl posed and photographed his dancing couple six times, and then printed each negative three times in order to achieve a cycle of eighteen images for his Phasmatrope.

Several inventors patented projects for sequence cameras: one of them, Wordsworth Donisthorpe, an English barrister, even proposed that the positive photographs thus achieved could be mounted on a flexible band for use in a projector. All these proposals were hamstrung by the inconveniences

 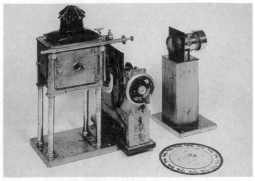

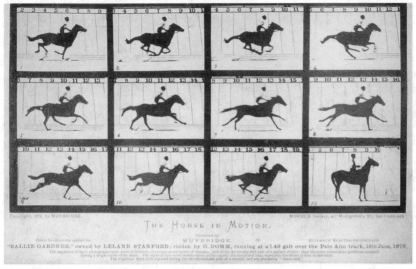

■ Eadweard Muybridge's photographic track at Leland Stanford's farm in Palo
Alto, California (above left). Twelve cameras mounted at the same height and distance apart were in the building at right. As the horse was ridden past, its legs tripped
a series of threads that activated the cameras and created a sequence of photographs
recording phases of the horse's movements. The wall at the left was painted to provide background and identity for each photograph. On June 19, 1878, Muybridge
took these photographs of Stanford's horse Sallie Gardner (above). Muybridge developed the Zoopraxiscope, a projecting Phenakistiscope, to show moving images of
horses and other animals (above right).

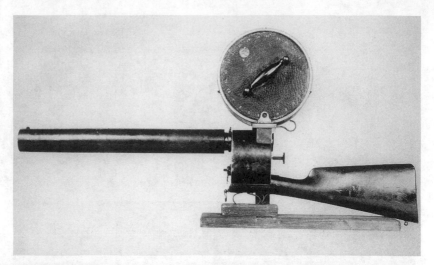

of the wet collodion process. The late 1870s however saw the development and marketing of the faster and more convenient gelatin bromide dry plate. This was to make possible the revolutionary achievements of Eadweard Muybridge (1830–1904), an English émigré who had already created a reputation as a photographer when he was commissioned by Leland Stanford, the railroad king and governor of California, to take "instantaneous" photographs of his racehorses, in order to establish whether a horse has all four feet off the ground simultaneously at a certain stage of the trot. Muybridge's first attempts, in May 1872, still with wet collodion plates, were reasonably successful, though the rapid exposures could only produce shadowy silhouettes.

The work was interrupted by Muybridge's arraignment (and subsequent acquittal on the grounds of justification) for the murder of his young wife's seducer, but in the summer of 1878 he resumed work at Sacramento. Now he placed a battery of twelve cameras alongside a specially prepared track.

PIECES IN A PUZZLE

■ Muybridge's pictures stimulated others to use photography to record and study movement. Etienne-Jules Marey's photographic gun, devised in 1882, and improved in several stages (facing page, above) generated an important analysis of bird, animal and human movement (facing page, below). Ottomar Anschütz's Electro-Tachyscope reconstructed animal movement from pictures arranged around the edge of a large glass disc and illuminated by intermittent flashes from a Geissler tube (left). Like Muybridge, horses figured strongly in Anschütz's work (below).

When the horse ran along the track, it broke a series of threads stretched across its path. Each thread in turn broke an electrical contact, and triggered the shutter of the next camera.

The resulting photographs attracted worldwide attention. In 1879 Muybridge increased the number of cameras to twenty-four and introduced a clockwork device to trigger them in even succession. Having thus analyzed movement, he experimented with resynthesizing it, by means of a large projecting phenakistiscope which he called the Zoopraxiscope. The projected images were not actual photographs: the series photographs were redrawn with some distortion to counteract the distortion produced by the projector.

Muybridge's photographs brought him world celebrity, and in 1881 he made a triumphant lecture tour of Europe, with his Zoopraxiscope. In Paris he met Etienne-Jules Marey, a French physiologist, who incidentally introduced Muybridge to the gelatin dry plate process, which in time gave him new possibilities. Marey, who had been making studies of animal locomotion by mechanical means, had already been in contact with Muybridge about the problems of recording birds in flight. Muybridge's equipment proved no solution, however.

Deciding to embark on the photographic method for himself, Marey revived an idea used by the astronomer Pierre-Jules-César Janssen in 1874. In order to photograph the passage of Venus across the sun, Janssen had built a "photographic revolver," in which a circular daguerreotype plate was revolved and intermittently exposed to record 48 images in 72 seconds. On similar principles, Marey in 1882 created a "photographic gun," which enabled him to follow and photograph the flight of birds. The following year he built a gigantic fixed-plate camera; but in 1888 he was able to announce a major step forward in his experiments thanks to the use of the new paper-based stripping film introduced by the Eastman Company for use in their new Kodak camera.

Other scientists and photographers were also stimulated by Muybridge's success to attempt "chronophotography." In Lissa, Ottomar Anschütz was commissioned to make studies of the Prussian cavalry. In Paris, Albert Londe used a single-plate, twelve-lens camera to study medical patients.

Anschütz subsequently commercialized a device, the Electro-Tachyscope, to reconstitute the movement he had recorded in his series photographs. The pictures, arranged as transparencies around the edge of a large wheel, were momentarily illuminated by flashes from a Geissler tube as they appeared in rapid succession before a viewing aperture.

Others however were already proposing devices for projecting moving photographs. Louis-Aimé-Augustin Le Prince, a Frenchman who had moved between England and the United States, appeared to have come very close to a solution with a roll-film machine patented in 1888: unhappily he disappeared mysteriously in 1890 before he could exploit his invention. William Friese-Greene, in England, was an enthusiastic but erratic experimenter, whose apparently overoptimistic claims to have solved the problems of photographing and projecting moving pictures may at least have served to stimulate others. Wordsworth Donisthorpe filed a new patent in 1889, but his ingenious proposals foundered for lack of commercial backing. Frederick Varley patented a stereoscopic sequence camera in 1890 (an almost identical design was patented by Friese-Greene three years later). In 1892 in France

Léon Bouly patented a dual-purpose apparatus called Cinématographe. All of these devices came close to putting together the pieces of the puzzle. Most had in common the lack of a satisfactory method of accurate registration of the successive frames—which would have been vital to effective projection.

This problem was to be solved triumphantly by the Edison Kinetoscope.

SORCERER AND APPRENTICE

Edison, Dickson, and the Kinetoscope

THE EDISON KINETOSCOPE MADE THE MOST SIGNIFICANT single step toward cinematography as we know it today. In its outward form the Kinetoscope appeared to descend from the ancient tradition of "peep shows"—boxes with mysterious apertures into which the spectator peered, to be rewarded with curious pictures. The difference was that the peepshow patrons of the eighteenth and nineteenth century had seen only static views. The picture in the Kinetoscope moved. Moreover, the images in the Kinetoscope were recorded on perforated, celluloid film of precisely the same format that is still current for motion picture projectors today. Only one piece in the motion picture puzzle was still lacking: the image was not yet projected. Yet the Kinetoscope viewer and its related camera, the Kinetograph, give Thomas Alva Edison a central place in the story of the cinema.

The true extent of Edison's personal contribution to the Kinetograph and Kinetoscope remains obscure, and a battleground for scholars. While most activities of the Edison laboratories are meticulously documented in papers preserved at the Edison National Historical Site at West Orange, New Jersey, the chronology and circumstances of the Kinetoscope's creation are confused. Vital documents are missing, while during long years of litigation over patent rights, personal recollections were conveniently revised and evidence was willfully distorted.

The contemporary picture is further complicated by Edison's own passion for publicity. During the Kinetoscope's years of gestation it seemed as if, whenever the project occurred to his mind or his laboratory reported some encouraging progress, Edison would seize upon any nearby newsman and discourse

■ Edison in Ore Milling Dept., Edison Lab. This portrait of America's most famous inventor, Thomas Alva Edison, was copyrighted by W. K. L. Dickson on June 20, 1893, at a time when Edison's motion picture machine, the Kinetoscope, was nearly complete. Dickson was head of ore milling research and development of the Kinetoscope, two projects that competed for his attention. Edison spent about $5 million in a futile effort to separate ore magnetically.

EDISON'S TELEPHONOSCOPE (TRANSMITS LIGHT AS WELL AS SOUND).

(Every evening, before going to bed, Pater- and Materfamilias set up an electric camera-obscura over their bedroom mantel-piece, and gladden their eyes with the sight of their Children at the Antipodes, and converse gaily with them through the wire.)

Paterfamilias (in Wilton Place). "BEATRICE, COME CLOSER, I WANT TO WHISPER." *Beatrice (from Ceylon).* "YES, PAPA DEAR."
Paterfamilias. "WHO IS THAT CHARMING YOUNG LADY PLAYING ON CHARLIE'S SIDE?"
Beatrice. "SHE'S JUST COME OVER FROM ENGLAND, PAPA. I'LL INTRODUCE YOU TO HER AS SOON AS THE GAME'S OVER?"

■ Edison's worldwide reputation as the originator of life-changing innovations inspired this English cartoon published December 9, 1878, in *Punch's Almanack for 1879*, almost ten years before Edison began serious work on the Kinetoscope and fourteen years before it was introduced to the public.

colorfully about his wonderful new living and talking pictures. Sometimes, for good measure, he would throw in a Far-Seeing (television) device. Newsmen and their readers enthusiastically lapped it up. Edison in his forties was already an American legend, the ideal Horatio Alger hero, the wizard who could transform Jules Verne's fantasies into everyman's present reality.

While the inspiration for experiments on moving pictures was no doubt Edison's—it was a natural concomitant of all his previous work in communications—the man most directly, practically, and certainly involved in the development of the Kinetoscope was Edison's assistant William Kennedy Laurie Dickson.

Dickson appears to have been born in Brittany, France, although his father was described as English and his mother was born to Scottish parents in

■ William Kennedy Laurie Dickson, Edison's photographic specialist, led the work to develop the Kinetoscope. He also designed the first movie studio where he produced, directed, and photographed the earliest motion pictures. This photograph shows him about 1902, at the peak of his career as partner-manager of the Mutoscope and Biograph Syndicate's London office.

Virginia. By February 1879 Dickson, his widowed mother, and his two sisters had evidently settled in Britain for on that date, then aged eighteen and a half, he wrote a letter from West Brompton, London, to Edison at Menlo Park. In this he declared his veneration, presenting himself as "a friendless and fatherless boy," although possessed of "patience, perseverance, an ardent love of science, and above all a firm reliance on God," and asking for employment. Edison (perhaps unimpressed by Dickson's spelling his name as `Eddison') sent a brief refusal. Three months later Dickson with his mother and two sisters emigrated to the United States; and four years after that, in the spring of 1883, he was finally given a job at the Edison laboratories, where he seems quickly to have proved himself a valuable assistant.

Dickson was a keen and accomplished photographer, as well as a resourceful inventor in his own right, and it was natural that Edison should assign him to the motion picture research. Edison provided the facilities, perhaps the impetus, and sometimes the vision; but there is now little doubt that all the experiment and practical work on the Kinetoscope were Dickson's.

"In the year 1887," Edison said years later, "the idea occurred to me that it was possible to devise an instrument which could do for the eye what the phonograph does for the ear." This date has been disputed by subsequent researchers, and it is certain that actual experiments began only later; but it seems quite likely that Edison's interest was aroused at this time by a spate of articles in the popular scientific press.

In the files of the Edison laboratory is a collection of relevant articles torn out of magazines and heavily marked and annotated. From *The Scientific American* of February 5, 1887, for instance, comes an article about collodion film and another by Marey about his and Muybridge's experiments in photographing movement. An article from *The Philadelphia Photographer* of June 4, 1887, on "Anschütz's Motion Pictures and the Stroboscopic Disk," by

Dr. P. Stolze, has many manuscript underlinings, particularly of passages discussing the rate of taking sequence pictures and the length of the picture series that had been achieved. A *Scientific American* article of August 2, 1887, on the Boula Telephone discusses the use of a continuous strip of sensitized paper to photograph electrical sound waves visually.

At this stage, however, Edison's interest in the problems could only have been speculative. He was deeply committed to costly experiments with an ore extraction process, which was also occupying Dickson, along with other laboratory assistants. Moreover the laboratory was in process of moving to a new site at West Orange which had been acquired early in 1887. The move was only nearing completion by the end of the year.

No doubt Edison's interest in motion pictures received a new stimulus when, on Saturday February 25, 1888, Eadweard Muybridge's lecture tours brought him to West Orange. Presumably his lecture included a demonstration of moving pictures produced by the zoopraxiscope. Edison and Dickson were almost certainly in the audience, and on the following Monday, February 27, a meeting was arranged between Edison and Muybridge. Muybridge subsequently (in the introduction to his *Animals in Motion*, 1899) claimed that on this occasion he "consulted with Mr. Thomas A. Edison as to the practicability of using [the zoopraxiscope] in association with the phonograph."

Eight months more, however, seem to have gone by before Edison gave serious attention to the project. On October 17, 1888, he filed with the Patents Office a "caveat," written nine days earlier. (A "caveat" is a description of an invention that the inventor wishes to develop further, or "mature," in the language of the Patents Office, before applying for a patent. The caveat is lodged in the confidential archives of the Patents Office, and acts as a bar to applications relating to the same invention, for the period of one year.) Edison's caveat declared "I am experimenting upon an instrument which does for the Eye what the phonograph does for the Ear, which is the recording and reproduction of things in motion. . . . The illusion is complete and we may see & hear a whole Opera as perfectly as if actually present although the actual performance may have taken place years before."

While this is an accurate prediction of the cinema of forty years later, the extremely vague and impractical technical proposals of the caveat show that Edison was still far from realizing it. At this stage he anticipated using a machine based on the mechanics of the phonograph, his favorite invention. He proposed that, just as the recording tracks were disposed on a phonograph, a series of microphotographs might be arranged in a spiral formation around a cylinder. He discussed as alternative possibilities both disk and continuous

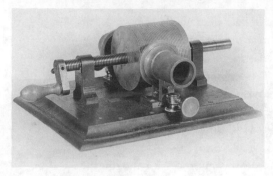

film, but rejected them as impracticable. Interestingly this first caveat also proposed that "the pictures may be even projected on the screen as in microphotographic projection or enlargement," although the means of achieving this—"the source of light inside of the cylinder"—seemed, to say the least, improbable.

In the week before the caveat was filed, Edison was canvassing scholarly lawyer friends for a suitable name for the proposed device. One of them suggested "Kinesigraph"; "Motograph" was dismissed as mixing Latin and Greek; and eventually, after Edison had browsed in Webster's dictionary, "Kinetoscope" was adopted.

Dickson was put in charge of experiments to realize Edison's proposal. Orders for supplies placed by the laboratory may provide some clue to his earliest researches, although such materials could equally have been used for other photographic activities regularly going on at the laboratory. A little mysteriously, sizable quantities of lantern slides were supplied by T. H. McAllister of New York, the best known stereopticon dealer of the day. About the same time a quantity of plates from Muybridge's mammoth publication *Animal Locomotion*, specially selected by Muybridge at Edison's request, arrived at the laboratory. In September 1888 microphotographic

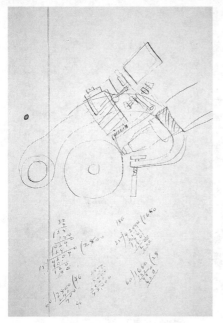

■ "I am experimenting upon an instrument which does for the Eye what the phonograph does for the Ear . . ." Edison's first motion picture caveat, October 17, 1888 (facing page left) announced that he was working on the Kinetoscope, a ". . . cheap, practical, and convenient" device to record and reproduce motion. He grandly predicted that future audiences would see and hear operas that had been performed years before. The drawings that accompanied the caveat (left) show that the concept for the motion picture machine was based upon the cylinder phonograph which Edison was redesigning for the commercial market at this time (facing page right).

lenses were ordered, although they were not delivered until March 1889, when they were found to have arrived in unsatisfactory condition from Zeiss in Germany; the defects were still not put right by June 1889.

By early 1889, however, work on the Kinetoscope was clearly accelerating. On January 31 the first charge was made to a separate Kinetoscope account; and four days later Edison wrote a second caveat, filed with the Patent Office on March 25. This referred to refinements of the cylinder machine—the provision of flat surfaces around the cylinder to avoid distortion of the individual microphotographs, and new details of a start-stop movement. Evidently the method of intermittent motion continued to give problems, because a third caveat, written on May 20 and filed on August 5, reverted to the idea of a continuously moving cylinder, with intermittent illumination by electric sparks.

The photographic medium too required some experiment. Edison's first caveat proposed coating the recording cylinder with photographic emulsion. This would however have been quite impractical, and Dickson was clearly seeking alternatives when, on November 28, 1888, he was recorded as going to New York to obtain supplies for the "daguerreotype experiment"—perhaps he was exploring the long outmoded daguerreotype process using silver-plated metal surfaces.

■ Serious experimentation on the Kinetoscope began during the summer of 1889, when a new photographic building was built at the Edison Laboratory in Orange, N.J. Most of the experimentation on the Kinetoscope took place in this building (above). The introduction of celluloid photographic film in 1889 was crucial to the final development of the motion picture. John Carbutt of Philadelphia sold photographic material that was transparent, flexible, and strong (right).

By the happy synchronism that so often marks the story of cinematography, however, at this very moment a suitable medium for the cylinder photographs made its appearance. In November 1888 John Carbutt announced that he had succeeded in producing photographic-quality celluloid in a uniform thickness of one hundredth of an inch. "Carbutt's Flexible Negative Films," the first emulsion-coated celluloid films, were marketed in 20" x 50" sheets by the Celluloid Manufacturing Company of neighboring Newark, New Jersey. On June 25, 1889 the Edison Laboratory ordered one dozen Carbutt films.

On August 2, 1889, with Dickson still proceeding with experiments on the cylinder moving picture machine, Edison sailed for Europe. In the course of his triumphal progress, he met Jules Marey; and the results achieved by Marey's roll-film chronophotographe, first demonstrated nine months before, were evidently to alter Edison's thinking and shake his faith in the cylinder solution.

On Sunday October 6, Edison returned from Paris, and the following day went to the laboratory where, in his absence, a new "Photographic Building" had been erected to accommodate Dickson's experiments. According to subsequent legend, Dickson welcomed his chief back with a demonstration of talking pictures projected on a screen.

Although Dickson never wavered in his account of it between 1894 and his death, forty-one years later, this remains the most mysterious and seemingly unlikely incident in the whole story of the Edison experiments. The event is supposed to have taken place at least a month before the first and unsatisfactory results of the cylinder device; seventeen months before the first showing of the Kinetoscope prototype; five years before the projection of motion pictures; and several years more before synchronization of sound and image passed beyond its most rudimentary stages. Even if we accept the subsequent evidence of Edison employees given in the course of patents litigation that the film strip mechanism was already in progress, it is hard to explain the claim of projection and synchronization.

Gordon Hendricks' relentless researches into *The Edison Motion Picture Myth* led him to the conclusion that Dickson had photographed some slides—perhaps by the painstaking single-shot method of Heyl—for use in an Anschütz Electro-Tachyscope. The Electro-Tachyscope had been widely publicized in the United States since 1887, and was certainly on sale by the autumn of 1889. Another Edison assistant, Eugene Lauste, later claimed he remembered an Electro-Tachyscope in the Photographic Building at this time. Hendricks' assumption that Dickson and his collaborators had rigged up the Anschütz device and a phonograph as a gag to amuse—and perhaps encourage—Edison remains at present, for want of other evidence, the most persuasive explanation.

No doubt Marey's progress gave Edison new stimulus. The use of a continuous band of film would have seemed to him a very natural solution, analogous as it was to the strips used in his earlier work on the telegraph and stock ticker. Moreover the new celluloid film base was being manufactured very close to home, in Newark. In late November 1889 he wrote a fourth motion picture caveat which was filed on December 16. Although this still mentioned microphotographs and intermittent illumination by electric sparks, Edison now proposed a continuous band of images on celluloid film, perforated with sprocket holes. Even before the caveat was filed, Dickson had ordered 54 lengths of film from the Eastman Company, who had begun to market their celluloid film that summer, in longer lengths than Carbutt's, and warned the factory that he would subsequently "require quite a number of these rolls."

By this time there was the added stimulus of apparent competition. On March 18, 1890, William Friese-Greene wrote from England to Edison, "Have sent you by same post a paper with description of Machine Camera for taking 10 a second which may be of interest to you. Yours faithfully, Friese-Greene." The article, "A Machine Camera Taking Ten Photographs a Second," which was reprinted in *The Scientific American*, is still in the Edison files. Clearly it was carefully studied at the laboratory. The tearsheet is heavily marked at certain phrases:

> . . . prepared film . . . a loop of fresh film into the exposed position . . . Mr. Friese-Greene thinks this machine camera to be likely to be useful for military purposes . . . Mr. Greene hopes to be able to reproduce upon the screen, by means of photographs taken with his machine camera, street scenes full of life and motion; also to represent a man making a speech, with all the changes in his countenance, and at the same time, to give the speech itself and the actual tones of the man's voice by means of a loud-speaking phonograph.

At the Edison laboratory they could hardly have guessed from such an optimistic report how far Friese-Greene was from a practical solution.

Even now work on the Kinetoscope seems not to have been a major priority at the laboratory; throughout the summer of 1890 both Edison and Dickson were still spending much of their time on the ore separation project, and there were no charges to the Kinetoscope account between May and November 1890.

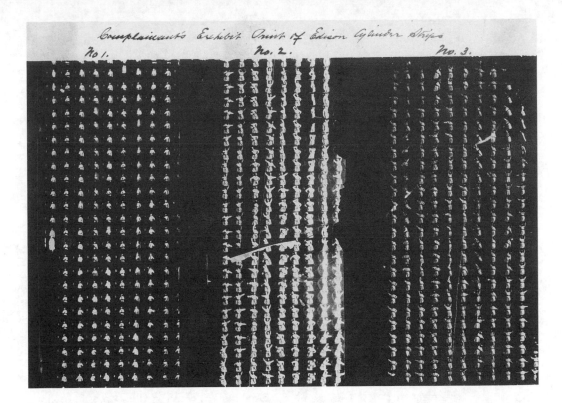

■   These strips of photographs, usually called "monkeyshines" were sent by Edison to the Patent Office in 1896, in support of his disputed application. They are the only surviving example of photographs made during Edison's early experiments with a phonograph-like cylinder.

In October 1890 however Edison found time to scribble some notes for a journalist, George Parsons Lathrop, whom he had agreed to assist with a work of science fiction. His vision of the future of the entertainment industry was eerily accurate: "Kinetoscope operas with phono every family wealth . . ." "Phono publishing houses kept star cos of actors & stage and produced for family use Kinetographic phonograms of whole Dramas and Operas. No theaters with actors in vogue."

Despite the apparent Friese-Greene threat and the new possibilities offered by flexible film, the cylinder experiments seem to have been carried on to the bitter end. Late in October 1890 a laboratory worker, Sacco Albanese, was paid a bonus of $1.50, apparently for dressing up and fooling around for the so-called "monkeyshines"—seemingly the first successful motion pictures produced by the cylinder machine. Photographic prints of this and two other films show that Dickson actually achieved results with the cylinder machine about this time; but it was clearly a dead end. The pictures could only be viewed by huge monocular magnification under which such microscopic images would have appeared impossibly grainy.

Perhaps indeed it was the evident shortcomings of these results achieved after two years of intermittent effort that convinced Edison and Dickson once and for all to abandon cylinders in favor of film. Again a clue to their preoccupations is afforded by the markings in an article, this time by Marey in *Contes Rendus* for November 1890. The phrases underlined include: "experiments . . . on a band of sensitised film exhibited on a luminous black ground . . . to obtain 10, or as many as 50 images a second . . . We can gather series of images in numbers varying from 30 to 120 . . . Balagny films are the most sensitive that I have found, but their length hardly exceeds 1m.10, they contain hardly 30 image-series."

Whoever marked the typescript translation in the laboratory files (and it seems most likely to have been Dickson or Edison himself) has particularly underlined the name of (Georges) Balagny, who had first introduced flexible film in France in 1886. (Earlier his paper stripping film had been licensed and manufactured by the French photographic firm of Lumière, which was later to play a significant role in the development of cinema.) Dickson himself went to a new film supplier in March 1891, buying film—most probably Blair's—from Merwin Brothers.

Even more significant is the heavy underlining and question mark beside the phrase, "images read from top to bottom." In the first version of the Kinetoscope, the images on the film were to be arranged sideways on the film.

Work evidently progressed very swiftly from this point. A particularly confident and effervescent interview with Edison appeared in the May 1891 issue of *The World's Columbian Exposition Illustrated*. He declared that thanks to an "improvement" on the phonograph he would shortly be able to project moving pictures. His additional prediction of television recalled a *Punch* cartoon of 1879, anticipating the Edison "telephonoscope."

Other newspapers published similar reports, and an *Electrical Engineer* article attributed to Edison a hazily imaginative account of the motion picture invention:

I make forty-six photographs a second on a moving sheet and by exhibiting this sheet moving at the same speed the scene is reproduced. I had a man sing into the phonograph the other day and I photographed him by this process as he was singing. Then I gave a concert. The

 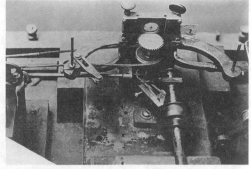

■ The working model of Edison's horizontal feed Kinetograph was ready by May 1891. The machine in these photographs was a "taking device" (camera), but it could be converted to a viewing machine by shining a light through the film and lens. This machine is the prototype of today's motion picture cameras and projectors.

The full view of the machine (above left) shows the lens (the tubelike cylinder) with a circular shutter in front of it (center). The electric motor is on the right (with gyroscope). The film was housed in circular metal cans mounted on spindles on either side of the aperture gate. Only one can is mounted on the machine as shown here. In use, it was covered by a wooden case that had an opening for the lens.

The close-up view (above right) shows the aperture gate of the horizontal feed Kinetograph with a strip of film in the machine. The aperture of this machine was round, so it took a circular image. The film was advanced by circular holes perforated along the bottom, which engaged with the sprocket teeth of the wheel in front of the aperture. The two canisters for film (not shown) were mounted on the spindles on either side of the aperture gate. One canister was filled with unexposed film, the other was empty to take-up the film after it was exposed in the aperture.

Two samples of film shot in the spring of 1891 are shown above. They are compared with a sample of a 35mm film made by Edison in 1900, which is like that used today (bottom). Note the difference in width, the circular image, and the horizontal orientation of the earlier film.

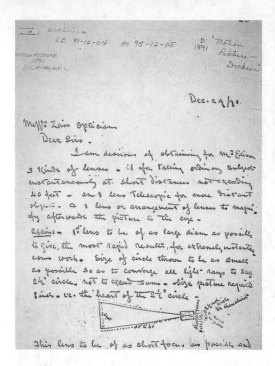

■ By December 1891, the Kinetoscope was taking shape. In a letter to William Zeiss, opticians in Rochester, N.Y., December 29, 1891, W. K. L. Dickson (for Edison) ordered three lenses. Two lenses for photography: a short focus lens for close, studio-type photography; a longer focus for distant photography. The third is a magnifying lens for viewing the film in a peep-show machine. He specifies lenses to photograph and view an image one inch wide—the size of today's 35mm film.

phonograph reproduced the singing and the Kinetograph reproduced all his motions and gesticulations.

The somewhat arbitrary number of 46 images (or "frames" as they would eventually be known) per second was to persist as the official standard speed for the Kinetoscope, although in practice it varied and was generally less than 40: the rate suggested in the four caveats had ranged from 10 to 25 pictures per second.

By the time that the *Electrical Engineer* article was published on May 20, 1891, the Kinetoscope prototype was ready—even if it was not exactly the sophisticated all-singing affair of which Edison had boasted. It was demonstrated for the very first time to a Convention of the National Federation of Women's Clubs, which Mrs. Edison invited to the laboratory on May 20. The event was reported in several newspapers, and from the description of the film

■ The Kinetoscope, Edison's coin-operated peep-show machine with the case closed (left) and open (right). The pictures were on a continuous ribbon of 35mm film threaded on rollers inside the box. The customer started the machine with a coin (a nickel or dime) and watched the film through a magnifying lens in an opening at the top. It stopped automatically after a single viewing.

exhibited we can be fairly certain that the device was the early, horizontal-feed version of the Kinetoscope, which is still preserved at West Orange along with a few fragments of film. (Gordon Hendricks suspected that the surviving model is a reconstruction made some years later, as supporting evidence in patents litigation.)

The mechanism was contained in a lightproof box and could serve both as camera and viewer, although in subsequent court evidence it was specifically referred to as a "taking device," i.e., camera. The film, 18mm wide (as against the subsequent standard width of 35mm) ran horizontally between two spools, at continuous speed. A rapidly moving shutter gave intermittent exposures when the apparatus was used as a camera, and intermittent glimpses of the positive print when it was used as a viewer—when the spectator looked through the same aperture that housed the camera lens. The mechanism was driven by an electric motor.

The strip of film most often described by early witnesses showed a half-length figure of Dickson facing the camera, bowing and raising his hat. Another film showed a young man swinging Indian clubs. Frames from these films were reproduced in a number of journals. The results clearly encouraged a new effort. We find Dickson selecting and ordering new lenses, and resuming his custom with the Eastman Company to order 50-foot rolls of Kodak film.

On August 24, 1891, patent specifications for the Kinetoscope and the Kinetograph were officially filed. Even now the cylinder idea was not entirely abandoned; one of the three applications still spoke of images on the surface of a drum illuminated intermittently by an electric spark.

The patent however shows that Dickson had now adopted the "top to bottom" arrangement of the film noted in the Marey article. Moreover the film width had been increased. In a letter of December 29, 1891, to Messrs Zeiss, opticians, ordering lenses for a new camera, he specifies: "Size of circle thrown to be as small as possible so as to converge all light rays to say 2 ½ in. circle. Not to exceed same—Size and picture required 1 inch—i.e., the heart of the 2 ½ in. circle." This indicates the use of 35mm film. This format, which was to remain the permanent standard for cinematograph film, was decided in a simple and arbitrary way. Eastman's Kodak film was supplied in 50-foot lengths, 2 ¾ in. (70mm) wide. The most convenient size for the Kinetoscope was achieved simply by splitting the Kodak rolls down the middle.

The prototype of the Kinetoscope in its ultimate form seems to have been ready in the late summer of 1892. It consisted of an upright wooden cabinet, 18 in. x 27 in. x 4 ft. high, with a peephole with magnifying lenses in the top. The oak casing was paneled, and in the eventual commercial models decorated with incised patterns.

Inside the box the film, in a continuous band of approximately 50 feet, was arranged around a series of spools. A large, electrically driven sprocket wheel at the top of the box engaged corresponding sprocket holes punched in the edges of the film, which was thus drawn under the lens at a continuous rate. Beneath the film was an electric lamp, and between the lamp and the film a revolving shutter with a narrow slit. As each frame passed under the lens, the shutter permitted a flash of light so brief that the frame appeared to be frozen. This rapid series of apparently still frames appeared, thanks to the persistence of vision phenomenon, as a moving image. The animation of photographs was accomplished.

FROM SCIENCE TO SHOW BUSINESS

Development of the Kinetoscope, as medium and commerce

FOR THOMAS EDISON INVENTION WAS NOT AN ABSTRACT, altruistic activity, it was his business. Experience both good and bad had taught him that there was a great deal of money to be made out of his creations, and that if he failed to make it himself, other people would do so for themselves. He had learned the importance of controlling manufacture, marketing, and licensing; at this very moment the exploitation of the phonograph in the entertainment industry was being actively explored and developed.

In June 1892 the eventual exploitation of the Kinetoscope on similar lines also must already have been under consideration, and Edison announced plans to have it ready for the World's Columbian Exposition in Chicago in 1893, the commemoration of the 400th anniversary of the coming of Columbus. This would, indeed, have been an auspicious launching for the Kinetoscope. The exhibition was above all a celebration of electricity, still a new marvel for most Americans; and Edison was the wizard and presiding genius of the electric art. The opening itself was to be a great coup de théâtre. In the White House, President Cleveland pressed the "magic button" that set in motion the great Allis machine in distant Chicago, whereupon the exhibition machinery started up and tens of thousands of lights blazed out.

Edison's private secretary and right-hand man, Alfred O. Tate, set up a consortium, with Thomas Lombard and a rich Omaha banker, Erastus Benson, to exploit the Kinetoscope at the Fair, and found his own enthusiasm matched by that of the Fair's organizers. Edison too was at first keen enough to loan the newly formed company, the Chicago Central Phonograph Company, $10,000, receiving in return a controlling interest and an undertaking

■ Chicago's World's Columbian Exposition, May–November 1893, celebrated the 400th anniversary of Columbus' voyage and demonstrated that Chicago had recovered from the disastrous fire of 1871. The Electric Building (right) was filled with wonders created by Edison, but although his Kinetoscope was announced as an attraction, the premiere was mysteriously delayed.

that he would be paid back from the first proceeds of the Kinetoscopes at the Fair. The consortium ordered 25 machines.

The Edison laboratory began preparations to fulfill the order. After rather severe handling by the examiners, who objected to many details which they said were not original to Edison, the patents for the Kinetograph camera and the Kinetoscope viewer were finally issued on February 21 and March 4, 1893, respectively. In April the prototype of the commercial version of the Kinetoscope was produced, and cabinets were ordered.

Clearly a considerable stock of films would be required to supply the Kinetoscopes planned for the Fair. Dickson seems to have perfected a satisfactory camera, the Kinetograph, by October 1892; and in December the building of a specially designed new studio was begun. From its supposed resemblance to a police wagon, the studio was forever afterwards to be

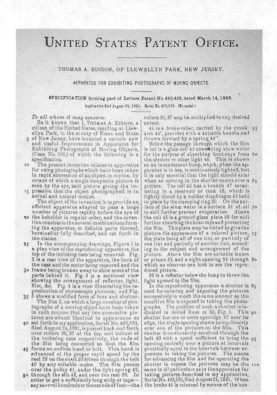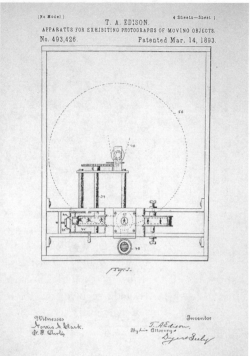

■ U.S. Patent 493,426, issued to Thomas A. Edison, for the Kinetoscope; page 1 (left) and sheet 1, a top view of the mechanism (right). In August 1891, Edison submitted three related patent applications. After several challenges and modifications, this patent for the peep-show machine was issued March 14, 1893. Edison used this patent for a camera and one issued later, to challenge his American competitors.

known as the Black Maria. Constructed of wood and tar paper, it was an elongated shed, with a roof that could be opened up to let in the sunlight. The whole building revolved on a pivot and circular rails so that it could be turned to take best advantage of the sunlight, though the facility was probably rarely used, since filming generally appears to have taken place at the same hour around midday. A reconstruction of the Black Maria stands to this day at the Edison National Historical Site in West Orange, though in a somewhat different location from the original.

The first official public demonstration of the Kinetoscope took place May 9, 1893, as part of a lecture by George Hopkins at the Brooklyn Institute of Arts and Sciences, where he was in charge of the physics department. Hopkins showed a number of lantern slides, concluding with a Beale

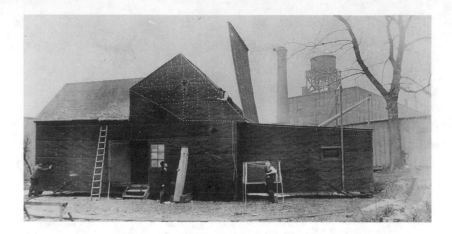

■ The first movie studio was a homely structure made of wood and tar paper. It was designed by W. K. L. Dickson and built on the grounds of the Edison Laboratory in Orange, N.J. in the winter of 1892–93. It amused Edison's staff, who dubbed it the "Black Maria" because it looked like a police wagon. Mounted on a pivot, it could be revolved and the roof opened to admit full sunlight on the subject being photographed.

Choreutoscope and a Ross Wheel of Life. After this he projected slides showing fragments of Kinetoscope film. The audience was then invited to file past the Kinetoscope, which Dickson had brought to Brooklyn, and take turns to view a film, *Blacksmith Scene*. The event was widely reported in the press.

Despite efforts at the laboratory and the protests of Tate, no Kinetoscopes were ready in time for the World's Fair, and the concession had to be surrendered. Problems had included Dickson's absence with a nervous breakdown, the alleged inebriety of the joiner, James Egan, who had been contracted to make the cabinets, and a lay-off of Edison workers. Speculation that a single Kinetoscope reached the Fair seems to be conclusively dismissed by an 1894 leaflet issued for the launching of the invention in London: "thousands of visitors to the Fair inquired daily at the Edison exhibits concerning the new machine . . . But great inventions take long time, extended experiment, and large expense before reaching practical and practicable perfection, and thus it was that the Kinetoscope was not perfected in time for the great Fair, and the anticipations of numberless people were for the time doomed to disappointment."

In August 1893 Dickson, who was accustomed to copyrighting his own still photographs, sent some "Edison Kinetoscopic Records" to the Library of Congress for copyright purposes. Unfortunately the original photographs have become detached from the copyright application and mislaid, so we do not know precisely the titles accorded the world's first motion picture copyright, No. 44,732Y. We do however know the subject of the next copyright, "No. 2,887Z—Edison Kinetoscopic Record of a Sneeze, January 7, 1894, deposited January 9, 1894." This brief subject, filmed a few days earlier, showed Fred Ott, a jovial Edison employee, sneezing violently. The "record" was made in response to a request from Barnet Phillips of *Harper's Weekly* for photographs to illustrate an article on "your wonderful Kinetograph. . . . Might I then ask if you would not kindly have some nice-looking young person perform a sneeze for the Kinetograph?" Phillips conveyed his request to Edison on October 31, 1893, but had to repeat it on January 2, 1894, whereupon Dickson evidently shot the film. Either the film was shot with an accompanying phonograph cylinder or Phillips had a vivid imagination, because his eventual article refers to hearing as well as seeing Ott's "explosive expiration."

Subsequent copyrights deposited by Dickson were "No.10,776Z—Edison Kinetoscopic Records, deposited April 9, 1894" and "No.10,777Z—Souvenir Strip of the Edison Kinetoscope, deposited May 18, 1894." This was, as the description suggests, not simply a positive print from film frames, but an advertising novelty to publicize a Kinetoscope film of the celebrated strong man, Eugene Sandow.

By the end of the year there was evidently a serious effort to produce Kinetoscopes to meet the order still outstanding from Tate and his associates. The bibulous Mr. Egan was replaced.

A fascinating aspect of the Kinetoscope era is that Edison's reputation and the prestige of his new invention enabled Dickson to persuade major figures from the world of show business to make the trip from New York to West Orange to appear in the Black Maria. Although the names of most of the performers are no longer familiar, for the vaudeville enthusiast of the nineties, the Kinetoscope repertoire was star-studded. It was a widely reported news event when in March 1893, Eugene Sandow, "The Strongest Man in the World," currently being promoted by Florenz Ziegfeld on a triumphant tour of American vaudeville theaters, appeared before the Kinetograph camera. The 27-year-old German waived his $250 fee for the privilege of meeting Edison. Lesser variety artists of the day recorded for the Kinetoscope included the Spanish dancer Carmencita, Annabelle Moore, who had appropriated the Butterfly Dance, which Loie Fuller had made famous in Europe, and the contortionist Madame Bertholdi. "Ruth Dennis, high kicker," was

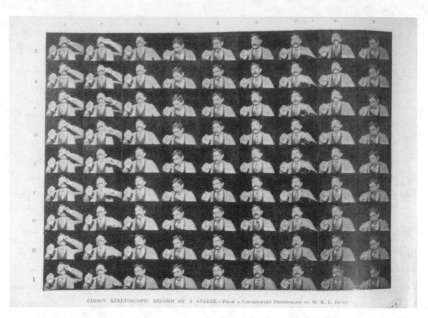

EDISON KINETOSCOPIC RECORD OF A SNEEZE.—From a Copyrighted Photograph by W. K. L. Dickson.

■ Dickson's second motion picture copyright was for *Edison Kinetoscopic Record of a Sneeze*, popularly called *The Sneeze*. Mailed on January 7, 1894, it was received at the Library of Congress on January 9, 1894, and registered the same day (below right). Dickson, who seems to have been careless about dates, misdated his letter January 7, 1893. He deposited a selection of frames from the movie mounted on cardboard and captioned in his own handwriting (facing page). These picturesque images of Edison employee Fred Ott taking snuff and sneezing have become one of the best-known icons of the early movies. It was reported that on his first intake of snuff, Fred Ott did not sneeze and the sequence had to be shot again—the first recorded retake.

The Sneeze was made at the request of Barnet Phillips, a writer for *Harper's Weekly,* for an article about the Kinetoscope that appeared in the March 24, 1894 issue. Frames from the film were reproduced in rows like the copyright application (above). Phillips numbered the top and put letters along the side to identify each frame. He characterized the nature of Ott's sneeze: A-1, the priming; C-2, the nascent sensation; G-2, the first distortion; A-8, oblivion; A-9, explosion, etc. He also mentions an accompanying sound recording. "Bless you, Mr. Ott!"

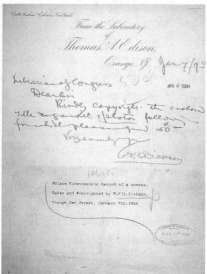

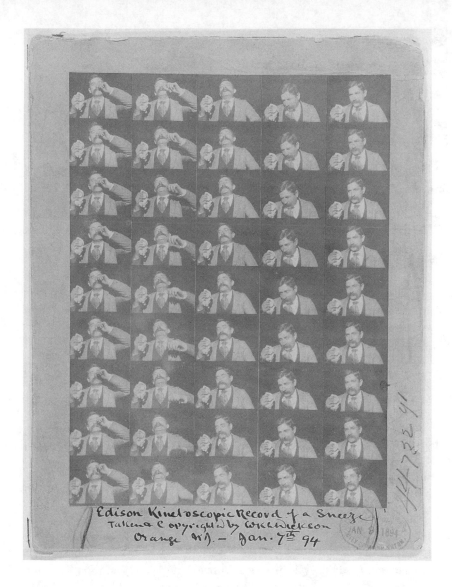

Edison Kinetoscopic Record of a Sneeze
Taken & Copyrighted by W.K.L.Dickson
Orange N.J. — Jan. 7th 94

later to achieve greater distinction as the pioneer of modern dance, Ruth St. Denis.

Although Sandow had a proven appeal to female audiences (in Chicago, society matrons paid up to $300 for the privilege of feeling his muscles) the repertory that was being built up appears already to have anticipated the predominantly male audience of peep show arcades. Along with the vaudeville acts and dancing girls were gymnasts, boxers, cockfights, and a film of terriers killing rats (not a huge success, it was reported, as the rats were too small). One of the

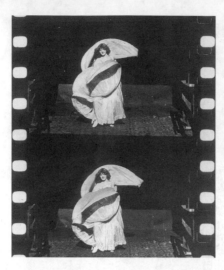

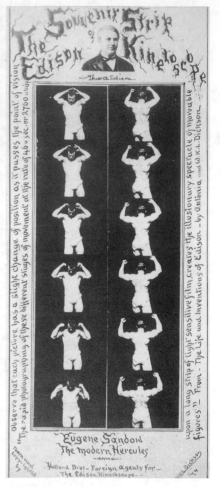

Popular stage personalities came to Edison's Laboratory to be filmed for the first movies. *The Souvenir Strip of the Edison Kinetoscope*, designed and decorated by W. K. L. Dickson, shows Eugene Sandow, "The Modern Hercules." Sandow, filmed in the Black Maria March 6, 1894 (right), was brought to the U.S. by Florenz Ziegfeld. His display of muscles, gymnastics, and flesh was popular with variety show audiences.

Annabelle Moore, "Peerless Annabelle—the Dancer," was filmed several times, the first in 1894. This imitation of Loie Fuller's popular *Serpentine Dance* was made in 1897 (above), but it is almost identical with the earlier film and was probably made to replace worn out copies.

more novel exhibits was a tooth extraction by Dr. Colton, who claimed to be the first dentist to administer gas. In the course of the next two years, performers from Barnum and Bailey's Circus and Buffalo Bill's Wild West Show—including Annie Oakley and Buffalo Bill Cody himself—would be filmed for the Kinetoscope. Later, too, scenes from successful stage productions—*Trilby*, *The South Before the War*, and *The Milk White Flag*—were filmed.

The notion of staging events specially for the cameras came early. For one of the very first films, *Blacksmith Scene*, an anvil was brought to the Black Maria stage, and workers from the technologically very sophisticated Edison machine room posed as simple smiths, pausing in their hammering to pass around a bottle. A barbershop scene showed a customer getting a lightning

Interior of Kinetoscope parlor at 1155 Broadway, near 28th Street, New York, operated by the Kinetoscope Co., controlling the United States and Canada. The first Kinetoscope exhibition started in the world; opened April 14, 1894.

■   The first Kinetoscope parlor opened at 1155 Broadway, New York City, April 14, 1894. It was owned by the Holland brothers, who were licensed by the Kinetoscope Company to distribute Kinetoscopes and Kinetoscope films in New York. Other investors opened parlors in cities across America almost as quickly as Edison could supply machines and films.

shave in the 20-second duration of the Kinetoscope reel. Occasionally the massive Kinetograph camera was taken outside the studio; the first time was on July 25, 1894, when the trapeze artist Juan Caicedo performed within the laboratory grounds.

On April 1, 1894, a new general manager, William E. Gilmore, took control of the Edison enterprises. A tough, abrasive figure, Gilmore brought a new, perhaps more professional, but certainly less sympathetic atmosphere to West Orange. Alfred O. Tate left a month after his arrival, and friction between Gilmore and Dickson seems also to have begun very quickly. One of Gilmore's first moves was to insist that the copyrights that Dickson had taken out in his own name be transferred to Edison, and this was effected on September 4.

On April 6, 1894, ten Kinetoscopes were finally ready for shipping to Holland brothers, at 1155 Broadway, New York, where the first Kinetoscope Parlor was opened on Saturday April 14. The premises had been a shoe store. The ten Kinetoscopes were arranged in two rows of five, with brass rails for the customers to lean on while viewing. There may be some license in a contemporary drawing which shows elegant customers of both sexes promenading among potted palms, but it is certain that a plaster bust of Edison, painted to look like bronze, stood in the window until Edison insisted on its removal, as lacking dignity.

The customers bought tickets for 25c, which permitted them to view all five machines in one of the two rows. Tate and his colleagues had planned to open the parlor on the following Monday, April 12, but the curiosity of passers-by persuaded them to advance the opening, and by the end of the first day they had grossed some $120. The films on show were *Sandow*, *Horse Shoeing*, *Barber Shop*, *Bertholdi (mouth support)*, *Wrestling*, *Bertholdi (table contortion)*, *Blacksmith Scene*, *Highland Dance*, *Trapeze*, and *Roosters*.

When ten more Kinetoscopes were ready in May, a second parlor was opened at 148 State Street, Chicago. The remaining five machines from the original order went to a San Francisco parlor opened on June 1 under the management of Peter Bacigalupi.

Kinetoscope parlors were now the rage, and opened up across the country as fast as the Edison Manufacturing Company, which had taken over production at the time of Gilmore's arrival, could supply machines. Marketing was handled by the original syndicate, now organized by Norman Charles Raff and Frank R. Gammon, and incorporated as the Kinetoscope Company.

A second group, the Kinetoscope Exhibition Company, was set up to market Kinetoscopes and films, by the apparently somewhat raffish brothers Gray and Otway Latham, with an associate, Enoch Rector. The Lathams perceived the attraction for the peep show public of prizefights, which were still against the law in most states. They persuaded the Edison Company to produce a special enlarged model of the Kinetoscope to accommodate films of 150 feet, and to slow down the film speed to 30 frames a second. In this way the running time of a film loop was extended to more than one minute. Their plan was to stage boxing matches in six one-minute rounds, and to exhibit the resulting films in a series of six machines. On June 14, 1894, the prizefighters Michael Leonard and Jack Cushing were brought to West Orange and fought before the Kinetograph. Early in August the Latham/Rector group opened a Kinetoscope parlor at 83 Nassau Street to show their Leonard–Cushing fight films. Customers paid 10c for each round, moving from machine to machine. Many however tended to save money by watching only the knockout round—which consequently was the film that most often had to be renewed.

These were censorious days. In July it was reported that Senator James A. Bradley, founder of Asbury Park, had objected to the exposure of Car-

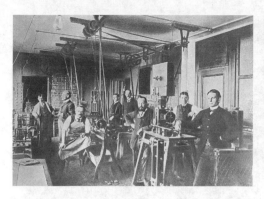

■ Filmed boxing matches stimulated the earliest large investments in the movie business. Gray and Otway Latham and their father, Woodville Latham (left), of the Kinetoscope Exhibition Company, persuaded Edison to enlarge the capacity of the Kinetoscope to approximate a round in a boxing match. The first fight filmed for them was the Leonard–Cushing fight, a six-round bout staged and filmed in the Black Maria on June 15, 1894 (right). Michael Leonard, a popular fighter was challenged by Jack Cushing. Rounds were limited to one minute and the ring, the stage area of the Black Maria, was smaller than normal. The filmed fight opened in August 1894, at the Latham's parlor at 83 Nassau Street, New York City.

mencita's stockinged ankles, and in August Robert Klenck of San Francisco was arrested for operating a Kinetoscope "alleged to be indecent." There were murmurings too in some newspaper reports against the showing of illegal prizefights in pictures.

New finance from a rich new partner, Samuel J. Tilden, enabled the Kinetoscope Exhibition Company to increase the number of their parlors and to embark on a much more ambitious fight project. On September 7, 1894, "Gentleman Jim" Corbett, who had taken the world heavyweight title from John L. Sullivan in 1892, came to the Black Maria and fought six rounds against a New Jersey fighter, Peter Courtney, who conveniently went down in the last one-minute round. Corbett was paid a royalty for each set of films put on exhibition, which eventually totaled more than $20,000.

The publicity surrounding the Corbett–Courtney fight started off a grand jury investigation, and Edison was subpoenaed. Although the newspapers had reported that he was the most enthusiastic spectator at the illegal meeting, he denied all knowledge and the case was quietly dropped.

The first year and a half of the Kinetoscope demonstrated not only that films could become big business, but also that they could command an international market. This was a possibility that Edison himself evidently failed to

■ *Corbett and Courtney Before the Kinetograph* (Edison 1894). The most ambitious Kinetoscope project was the six-round match between the heavyweight champion "Gentleman Jim" Corbett and challenger Peter Courtney. The fight was staged in the Black Maria September 7, 1894, before an audience of Edison employees and a contingent of journalists who recorded the event at length. The filmed fight premiered in New York in late September 1894.

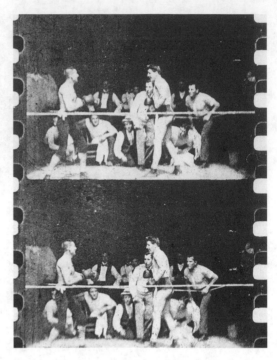

predict, since he neglected to take out foreign patents on the Kinetoscope and Kinetograph. The potential was perceived, however, by Joseph D. Baucus and Frank Z. Maguire, who have historic roles as the first men to open up the American cinema's vital international market. In September 1894, along with a rich young associate, Irving T. Bush, they established the Continental Commerce Company in New York City at 44 Pine Street, with exclusive rights to exploit the Kinetoscope abroad. Their first foreign parlor was opened on October 17 in a shop below their offices at 70 Oxford Street, London, where they also established their European headquarters. The score of films shipped for this occasion included *Horse Shoeing*, *Blacksmith Scene*, *Cock Fight*, *Barber Shop*, *Wrestling Match*, *Highland Dance*, and *Bar Room*, two Madame Bertholdi films, three Annabelle films, and *Carmencita*.

The London opening was widely and enthusiastically covered by the press. The writers were impressed by such details as the smoke rising from the blacksmith's forge or from a pipe, and the changing expressions of the people in the films. The *Daily Telegraph* reported with awe that "the actors in some cases disappear from the stage and then return."

A little surprisingly, given that the Continental Commerce Company had its headquarters in London, Paris seems to have seen the Kinetoscope rather

The Kinetoscope was marketed in Europe a few months after it opened in New York. This stylish poster was made for Casimir Sivan & Co., Geneva, Switzerland.

earlier. Mysteriously, a single Kinetoscope arrived in Paris and was put on display, along with a phonograph, in the dispatch room of the journal *Le Petit Parisien*. Readers of *La Nature* were informed in the issue of October 20 that "Messrs Werner Brothers, Edison's Paris representatives, have installed several Kinetoscopes in premises at 20 Boulevard Poissonière, where they operate all day and evenings." The Paris proprietors were Michel and Eugène Werner, who seem never to have been fortunate in business enterprises which moved capriciously from typewriters to Kinetoscopes and thence to bicycles. Their film repertoire seems more or less to have duplicated that of London. In general the Parisians seemed less disposed than the English to admire. One critic considered it a shortcoming that the images lacked color. An article in *La Nature*, some weeks before the arrival of the Kinetoscope, sniffed that Marey, Muybridge, Anschütz, and Londe had all anticipated Edison: "these devices have absolutely nothing new for us . . . the only new and interesting aspect of the invention is that the duration of the phenomenon or scene that passes under our eyes is 50 seconds . . . Once again the Americans do it *big*."

Records of the Continental Commerce Company's other European ventures are elusive. We know that the Kinetoscope was shown in Geneva, where the agents were Casimir Sivan and Company, and in various Italian cities. In London the company advertised that "The Edison Kinetoscope as a money-maker has never been equaled. Machines have been earning from 750 to 1,000 percent. on the investment." The Paris agents were more conservative, estimating that its exhibition could bring back 500 percent on the capital investment. For the moment such optimism seemed justified. Kinetoscopes were a craze; within a few months five new exhibitions had opened in London, and new parlors continued to open throughout the United States.

Success brought imitation. At home, a former Edison employee, Charles Chinnock, produced a motion picture camera and a Kinetoscope device which was exhibited publicly from January 1895. On November 21, 1894, a patent application for a peep show device on quite different principles, the Mutoscope, was filed, and its inventor, Herman Casler, was working on the design of a camera, which would become the Biograph. From London the Continental Commerce Company reported with alarm that a London instrument maker, Robert W. Paul, was already supplying the European market with Kinetoscopes of his own manufacture.

But by the end of 1894 it was clear that the brief Kinetoscope craze and boom was fast coming to an end. Sales of machines and films fell rapidly and dramatically. Once the novelty value had worn off, the curious voyeuristic experience of peep show parlors could attract only a very limited audience.

The Edison concern attempted to stimulate the market by fulfilling Edison's original promise of combining the Kinetoscope and the phonograph. No doubt experiments in synchronization had continued: Edison and Dickson's public statements on the Kinetograph and Kinetoscope rarely failed to make some mention of sound. An interesting little film of uncertain date (perhaps 1893) may well represent a kineto-phonographic experiment. This shows Dickson himself playing a violin in front of a huge phonograph horn while two young male Edison workers solemnly dance cheek to cheek. An article in *Leslie's Monthly* by Dickson's sister, Antonia, which was subsequently reworked to make both a small booklet, *History of the Kinetograph, Kinetoscope, and Kineto-Phonograph*, and a chapter in the Dicksons' *Edison, His Life and Inventions*, claimed:

> The phonograph is now mechanically and electrically linked with a specially constructed camera . . . Thus, when reproduced, the minutiae of expression or gesture will be found to be harmoniously combined with their appropriate gradations of sound even to the delicate inflections of the lips in molding speech or song.

On March 16 *The Orange Chronicle*, evidently inspired by a laboratory press release, announced the imminence of

■ An Edison experimental sound film. A test film was shot in the Black Maria at an unknown date. Two self-conscious Edison employees dance while W. K. L. Dickson plays the violin into the recording horn of a phonograph. Edison frequently spoke about combining the phonograph with the motion picture, but the Kinetophone was not marketed until 1895, when the Kinetoscope business was dwindling.

another novelty . . . from the fertile brain of Thomas A. Edison and his gifted lieutenant, William K. L. Dickson . . . It is the connection of the kinetoscope with the phonograph in such a way that the two will work synchronously and the vocal expression exactly keep pace and follow the visual expressions . . . It will for instance be possible to take a reproduction of an entire opera.

As usual these reports extravagantly exaggerate the Edison achievement in matching sound and vision. The Kinetophone, which was eventually put on sale in March 1895, made no attempt at synchronization. The viewer listened through tubes to a phonograph concealed in the cabinet and performing approximately appropriate music or other sound. The first Kinetophones seem to have been available in April. Customers who already had Kinetoscopes could buy a conversion outfit that enabled them to insert a phonograph attachment in their existing machines—an indication of the lack of any attempt at synchronization.

The Kinetophone failed to prolong the career of the Kinetoscope: only 45 machines were sold. A few Kinetoscopes lingered in amusement arcades around the world into the start of the new century, but the peep show had now to give way to projected moving pictures. The puzzle was finally to be completed.

THE RACE TO THE SCREEN

Projecting the motion picture

THE EDISON KINETOSCOPE WAS AT ONCE AN ADVANCE and a hiatus in the development of motion pictures. Practically all the photographic moving picture devices that had preceded it anticipated projection of the images; and projection was vaguely discussed during most of the Kinetoscope's career. Yet, apocryphally, Edison is said to have positively opposed the idea. Terry Ramsaye, whose 1925 history of American motion pictures, *A Million and One Nights*, is a frustratingly undifferentiated mixture of unique record and lurid journalistic color, alleges that Edison replied to proposals to develop a projecting machine:

> No . . . if we make this screen machine that you are asking for, it will spoil everything. We are making these peep show machines and selling a lot of them at a good profit. If we put out a screen machine there will be a use for maybe about ten of them in the whole United States. With that many screen machines you could show the pictures to everyone in the country—and then it would be done. Let's not kill the goose that lays the golden egg.

Edison wrote a laudatory preface to Ramsaye's book and had the opportunity to approve it, so there may be some substance in this account. On the other hand Ramsaye also says that growing rancor between Dickson and his employer was aggravated when Dickson learned that his colleague Charles Kayser had secretly been put to work to develop a projection apparatus. It is certain, however, that Dickson himself had no official encouragement to pursue this line of progress at the laboratory.

The Latham brothers and their scholarly father, Woodville, however, clearly had a sense of show business as well as enterprise, and reasonably estimated that their prizefight pictures would fare better with an audience than when viewed by solitary voyeurs. They were joined by Eugene Lauste, a former Edison employee, whom Dickson (according to his evidence in subsequent patents litigation) appears to have recommended in response to a request for advice about a good mechanic.

The formal character of Dickson's own association with the Lathams is hard to define. His inventive enthusiasm undoubtedly led him into outside associations while he was still in Edison's employ: he had an informal relationship with his friend Henry Marvin that later resulted in the K.M.C.D. Company and eventually the American Mutoscope Company. The Portable Electric Light and Power Company of Orange marketed a mining lamp, which Dickson had patented. In later years, Dickson denied any formal relationship with the Lathams or their Lambda Company; they had, he said, given him some Lambda stock without solicitation, and because of his own uncertainty about his future with Edison this stock was held in his attorney's name.

He had first met and liked the Lathams as Edison clients. Late in 1894, he said, they sought his advice about approaching Edison for projection rights in the Kinetoscope. Dickson alleged that Edison declined to go into business with them and shrugged off the affair.

Dickson himself said that his dislike of their business style dissuaded him from any formal partnership with the Lathams, although he admitted working on their first test film (of a light bulb) while still working for Edison, and filming the Griffo–Barnet fight film on May 4, 1895, after leaving Edison.

Whatever the nature of his association with the Lathams, however, it led to his ultimate parting from Edison. Much later Dickson alleged that he had been used to carry out espionage on behalf of Edison, to ascertain the Lathams' intentions, but that "all this & much more was purposely misinterpreted by one evil-minded man (so as I since thought) to appropriate my big interests of 10%—it looked so anyway."

The "evil-minded man" was, of course, William E. Gilmore. Whatever the precise facts, it seems evident that early in 1895 there was a confrontation with Gilmore, as a result of which Dickson, indignant that his loyalty should be impugned, resigned forthwith from the Edison concern on April 2, 1895.

Meanwhile Lauste had constructed a camera with an intermittent film movement. In contriving a projector, however, Lauste and the Lathams followed the Kinetoscope plan of continuously moving film with a synchro-

■ Edison was firm in his commitment to the peep show machine and rivals began to design projectors to compete with him. The Lathams developed their projector, the Eidoloscope in 1895, after seeking advice and assistance from W. K. L. Dickson. It evaded Edison's patents by using wider film. By May 1895, the Lathams were projecting film of a boxing match in a storefront theater in New York City.

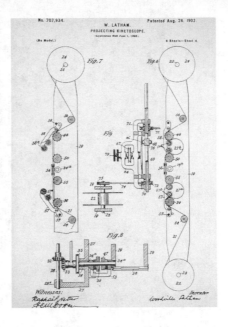

nized shutter to provide rapid intermittent illumination. To offset the resulting problem of limited illumination, a film width of two inches—larger than the Edison gauge—was adopted.

There were other significant variations from the Kinetoscope: the film was run from one spool to another, rather than in an endless band, and moved upwards, from the lower to the upper spool—the opposite direction from Kinetoscope film. One aspect of the projector was to have quite disproportionate significance in years to come. To avoid undue strain on the film from the inertia of the heavy spools, an additional feed sprocket served to maintain a loop of slack film from which the intermittent movement was supplied, to avoid jerking the entire reel. This device was to become famous, or infamous, as "the Latham Loop."

On April 21, 1895, the Lathams arranged a demonstration of this Panoptikon Projector at their workshop in Frankfort Street, New York. The press was mildly favorable although reporters mischievously solicited some rather threatening comments from Edison. Undeterred, on May 4 the Lathams shot an 8-minute film of a fight between "Young Griffo" and Charles Barnett, and on May 20, 1895, opened a storefront theater at 156 Broadway in which to show it. By the end of the month the projector—now renamed the Eidoloscope—was presented as a vaudeville turn at the Olympic Theater, Chicago.

Dickson's associations outside the Edison laboratory were not confined to the Lathams. He appears to have passed on an idea for a cheap and

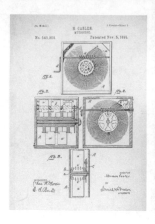

■ The K.M.C.D. syndicate in Canastota, N.Y., September 1895. Left to right: Henry N. Marvin, W. K. L. Dickson, Herman Casler, and Elias B. Koopman. The initials of their surnames gave the syndicate its name. This group established the well-financed American Mutoscope Company, which became Edison's chief American rival. Their peep show machine, the Mutoscope (above right), was a simple and very sturdy device. Photographed images printed on a firm bromide paper were mounted around a drum. The viewer turned a crank attached to a worm gear revolving the drum. The photographs were viewed through an aperture. It was designed to avoid competing with Edison's patents.

simple alternative to the Kinetoscope to an engineer friend, Henry Norton Marvin, and his partner, Herman Casler, another former Edison employee. Dickson's new proposal was an elaboration of the principle of a flick-book, using series of photographs mounted on cards. In the device as perfected and patented (as the Mutoscope) by Herman Casler, the sequence photographs were arranged around the perimeter of a drum. When the drum was revolved in a specially arranged cabinet, the cards were rapidly flipped before the eye, giving an impression of movement. The charm of the device was that it required no special illumination or electric motor: the viewer could control and vary the speed as wished, simply by turning a handle.

On November 21, 1894, Casler filed a patent application for the device under the name of Mutoscope. By March 1, 1895, he was able to offer his partners, who now included a businessman, Elias Koopman, a demonstration of a

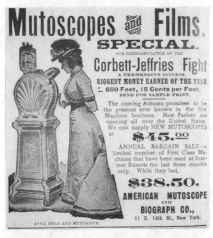

■ In 1900, The American Mutoscope Company hired Anna Held, the popular Ziegfeld star, to appear in ads for the Mutoscope (above left). She is shown standing and peering into the viewing aperture of the decorated iron model used in arcades (above right) and with a smaller table top version (center left). She might be looking at herself because she also appeared in one of the company's films (below left).

camera, subsequently called the Biograph, to take views for the Mutoscope. By early June the camera was in operation, After leaving Edison, Dickson seems to have spent his summer at Canastota, New York, where the Marvin–Casler concern was located, and probably was responsible for shooting the first films.

■ One of the earliest motion picture projectors was the Phantoscope, designed by Thomas Armat (above left) and C. Francis Jenkins (above right). It was an improved version of a peep show machine developed by Jenkins. The Phantoscope premiered at a booth next to the Old Plantation at the Cotton States Exposition (above) in Atlanta, Georgia, in late September 1895. Their projector was destroyed by a fire, which started in the Old Plantation. A month later the partnership dissolved after a disagreement and Armat and Jenkins became bitter rivals.

On November 5, 1895, the Mutoscope patent was issued and on November 14 application was made for a handheld Mutoscope. The same month the Mutoscope was adapted, with the use of a mirror device, to project motion pictures, a demonstration was reported as taking place in Mahon's machine shop in Canastota. Soon afterward the group perfected a through-the-film projector, the Biograph.

On December 27 the American Mutoscope Company was established, the partners being Dickson, Casler, Marvin, and Koopman. In January 1896 Casler's patents rights and outstanding applications were assigned to the company, which now set up premises at 841 Broadway, New York. On February 26 a patent was filed for the Casler camera.

In March 1895 C. Francis Jenkins, a young government clerk in Washington who had invented a variant on the Kinetoscope (which he called the Phantoscope), entered an agreement with Thomas Armat, a fellow student at the Bliss School of Electricity, to develop a motion picture projection device. On May 28, 1895, the two partners entered a new patent application for a Phantoscope projector; and in September of the same year gave public demonstrations at the Cotton States Exposition in Atlanta. There is no evidence of the quality of the results. Soon afterward the partners seem to have disagreed and split up, each claiming the invention as his own.

Jenkins had his projecting Phantoscope ready by the end of the first week of November 1895, and on December 12 demonstrated it at the Franklin Institute in Philadelphia. Almost simultaneously, Armat demonstrated his version of the Phantoscope to Raff and Gammon, who were enthusiastic, and negotiated to secure Edison and Gilmore's agreement to develop the machine. In February 1896 it was given a new name, Vitascope, with the significant addition of "Edison's." Raff and Gammon persuaded all the parties concerned that Edison's name was essential to the effective publicity and exploitation of the device. On February 27 Edison attended a demonstration of "his" Vitascope. To judge from the news reports, he played the role of its inventor with great aplomb.

Meanwhile there was no less energetic motion picture activity in Europe. Robert William Paul, an instrument maker of Hatton Garden, London, was approached in late 1894 by two Greek entrepreneurs who asked him to build copies of the Edison Kinetoscope. Paul was reluctant until he discovered to his delight that there was no British patent to be breached. He began to manufacture Kinetoscopes, and quickly set to work with the collaboration of Birt

■ "... a new screen machine." The novelty of the Kinetoscope soon wore off and showmen were anxious to project movies. Edison did not have a projector so Raff and Gammon wrote Edison's business manager, William E. Gilmore, recommending Thomas Armat's version of the Phantoscope as the best machine to project Edison films. After a successful demonstration for Edison, the Phantoscope was renamed the Edison Vitascope.

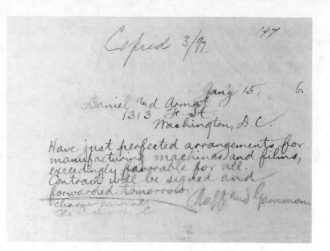

Acres, a photographer, to make a camera to supply films for the device. The prototype was ready by March 1, 1895, and by March 29 Paul was successful and confident enough to send samples of his films to Edison with a proposal that they might arrange some form of exchange. Edison replied that this was not practicable since he made his films only to the order of outside entrepreneurs.

Like Jenkins and Armat, Paul and Acres quickly disagreed and went their separate ways. On May 27, 1895, Acres patented his Kinetic camera, and two days later filmed the Derby at Epsom, although apparently still using the original camera developed with Paul. In June and July he was in Germany to film the ceremonies of the opening of the Kiel Canal.

Paul was a man of vision. On October 4 he took out a patent for an entertainment in which motion pictures would be used to give spectators the illusion that they were taking part in a Time Machine expedition. The patent proposed—as an essential element in the show—the use of a projection device incorporating intermittent movement of the film.

Now rivals, Paul and Acres embarked on their own race to develop a projector. On January 14, 1896, Acres gave the first film projection in Britain at a meeting of the Royal Photographic Society at 12 Hanover Square. In February Paul published details of his projector, the Theatrograph.

In Lyons, France, Antoine Lumière had stirred the interest of his sons Louis and Auguste Lumière in the problem of motion pictures. The manager of their family-run photographic goods factory later recalled, "In the summer of 1894 father came into my office where I was with Louis, and

■ Louis and Auguste Lumière, optical and photographic manufacturers in Lyons, France, were intrigued by the business possibilities the Kinetoscope offered. Using it as a model, they built the Cinématographe, a versatile, compact machine which could be used as camera and projector.

took out of his pocket a piece of Kinetoscope film which had been given him by one of the Edison concessionaires, and said to Louis, precisely: 'This is what you have to make, because Edison sells this at crazy prices and the concessionaires are trying to make films here in France to have them cheaper.' "

The brothers worked on the idea through the winter. Auguste made the first experiments; Louis proposed an intermittent mechanism based on the movement of a sewing machine; and on February 13, 1895, the Cinématographe was patented in their joint names. With the resources of their factory behind them, they constructed a machine which still commands admiration for its lightness, elegance, and efficiency. Hardly bigger than an ordinary hand camera, and with a mechanism that purred, the Cinématographe served a triple function of camera, printer, and projector.

Unlike Edison, the Lumières were quick to patent the Cinématographe in other countries; the English patent was taken out on April 8, 1895. Throughout the rest of that year the Lumières skillfully publicized their invention through a series of strategically planned shows, generally for learned societies in France and Belgium. The public thus had plenty of opportunity to read about the marvelous Cinématographe before the day, December 28, 1895, when the Lumières began regular screenings for paying audiences in the basement of the Grand Café, Boulevard des Capucines.

Early in 1896, an old friend of Lumière père, the vaudeville performer Félicien Trewey—an exponent of "chapeaugraphy" and "shadowgraphy"—took the Cinématographe to London. Here he found himself neck and neck with Paul and Acres. On February 20, the same day that Trewey first showed the Lumière Cinématographe at Marlborough Hall, Regent Street, Paul gave a demonstration of the Theatrograph at Finsbury Technical College, London, and on March 2 patented an improved model of his apparatus.

The success of the Marlborough Hall shows brought Trewey an engagement at the Empire Leicester Square, London's leading music hall. Opening on March 9, the Cinématographe proved so popular that in addition to its presentation in the regular evening program, special matinee demonstrations were given in the grand foyer of the theater.

Animated photographs were suddenly the rage of London. On March 19, 1896, the celebrated illusionist David Devant exhibited Paul's Theatrograph at the Egyptian Hall; two days later Paul launched a much-publicized show at Olympia Exhibition Center; and the same day Birt Acres began exhibitions of his Kineopticon in a small hall in Piccadilly. Paul's Olympia show attracted the attention of the managers of the Alhambra, Leicester Square, who did not intend to be outdone by their nearby rival, the Empire. Paul's projector, now renamed the Animatograph, opened at the Alhambra on March 25. A third British-made projection device, Riggs' Kinematograph, opened at the Royal Aquarium, Westminster, on April 6.

Throughout the succeeding months, vaudeville theaters around Britain competed fiercely for moving picture acts. The Cinématographe was far ahead of the rest in traveling the British Isles. By April 20 it was at the Star Theatre of Varieties in Dublin. During May and June it reached Newcastle-upon-Tyne (the Art Gallery), Cardiff, Manchester, Edinburgh, Glasgow, Hull, Bristol, Newcastle-upon-Tyne again, this time to play the Empire Theatre of Varieties, Leicester and Sheffield. The Animatograph's first recorded engagement outside London was on June 8 when it played the Tivoli, Bristol, with a program largely made up of Edison films. On June 22 it opened at the Assembly Rooms, Bath. Paul and Lumière were not the only showmen exploiting films in these first months. A mysterious Fred Harvard was touring with what he variously described as his Animatoscope, Cinématoscope, or Cenematoscope around provincial music halls from the beginning of May 1896, and a Vincent Paul was reported as bringing "the latest wonder (the cinématographe) for the first time to Liverpool" on May 18, 1896.

The French and English inventors were competitors in the race to American screens, although the victory finally went to the Edison Vitascope. The first theatrical exhibition took place on April 23, 1896, at Koster and Bial's Music Hall in Herald Square, New York City, advertised, naturally, as "Edison's

Latest Marvel." Two machines were used, stationed in a booth in the grand circle, and draped with velvet to match the furnishings of the theater. The screen, lowered from the flies, was set in an elaborate gilt picture frame. As in the Kinetoscope, the films were arranged as continuous loops in spoolbanks, so that each one could be repeated for as long as was desired, which helped to avoid breaks in the show for changing the film.

Ironically, delighted as the audience was with the umbrella dance, a boxing bout, *The Milk White Flag*, and a hand-colored Annabelle skirt dance, the film that made the greatest impression on audience and reviewers alike was a film by Robert Paul, *Rough Sea at Dover*, which somehow had fallen into the hands of Raff and Gammon. It is hard today to comprehend the full impact on audiences of 1896 of their first exposure to motion pictures. Their amazement that even details like leaves on trees moved shows what a great jump it was from the mechanically produced moving images in the magic lantern. Reports of the physical shock upon spectators are frequent enough to be credible. *The Optical Magic Lantern Journal* reported in June 1897 that the realism of Paul's *Rough Sea at Dover* was

> so great that a shudder can hardly be supressed and the splash can be easily imagined. In another [film], where a turn out of a fire engine was being shown, the engine dashes down the street towards the audience and appears to come right upon them. On one occasion, an old lady in the audience, quite unable to suppress a scream, started up in her seat and tried to scramble out, and in doing so knocked over the person behind her in her endeavor to get away from the horses; many more cases of the same sort have been known.

The rival shows soon followed the Vitascope into New York. The arrival of the Vitascope spurred the Latham group to introduce an intermittent mechanism into the Eidoloscope, and on May 11, 1896, the improved machine secured a vaudeville engagement at the Olympia Music Hall, Manhattan.

On June 29 the Lumière Cinématographe opened at Keith's Union Square Theater, and for a time its exotic and more sophisticated repertoire of films, along with the impeccable photographic and projection quality that the Lumière machine offered, bid fair to eclipse the Vitascope. On August 24 Birt Acres' Kineopticon opened at Tony Pastor's Theater.

Although a latecomer, the most serious rival to all the rest was to be the Biograph. Projector and films were ready to be launched in a touring show, *Sandow's Olympia*, which opened on September 14 in Pittsburgh. The tour continued through Philadelphia and Brooklyn, and the show arrived at

■ *Milk White Flag* was one of the films presented by Raff and Gammon in the first Vitascope program at Koster and Bial's Music Hall. Members of the Broadway cast were photographed in the Black Maria in 1894.

Hammerstein's Grand Opera House, New York, on October 5. The larger film (the frame was four times the size of the Edison standard) gave a much bigger, brighter, clearer, and steadier picture than any of its rivals. Dickson had moreover devised the program cunningly. The theatrical extracts included the kiss scene from *Trilby and Little Billee*, and the well-loved Joseph Jefferson in his famous role as Rip Van Winkle (Jefferson's son was the impresario of *Sandow's Olympia*). Scenes of presidential candidate McKinley ensured enthusiastic reception from Republicans, who turned the showings into virtual political rallies; and shots of the Empire State Express rushing by—positively frightening on the giant screen—attracted patronage from the railroad company.

From Hammerstein's, the Biograph moved to Koster and Bials, and on January 1897 began a run at Union Square Theater that was to last, apart from one four-month gap, until July 15, 1905. (Long runs seemed characteristic of the Biograph. At the Palace Theatre, London, it remained on the bill from 1897 to 1900.) By Christmas 1896 the Biograph was playing in at least six vaudeville houses.

From the summer of 1896 the competing projection devices were being exploited in vaudeville theaters across the states. Exploitation of the Vitascope was organized on lines that had already been developed profitably (for Edison) for the phonograph. Territorial rights were sold off to individual entrepreneurs, who seem rarely to have done well out of the deal, largely because of the problems of exploiting an all-electric machine at a period when electricity supplies were still uncertain.

Showmen were meanwhile experimenting with other forms of exhibition. In London, Trewey at the Marlborough Hall and Acres in Piccadilly had already tried out the idea of shows made up of films alone, rather than

128

■ The rooftop studio of the American Mutoscope Company at 841 Broadway, New York City (above). After leaving Edison for American Mutoscope, W. K. L. Dickson (second from right) designed and built this outdoor studio on the roof of the company's office building near Union Square. He is standing with unidentified officers of the company on the stage. The Mutograph camera was housed in the movable shed (above) and like Dickson's Black Maria, the stage could pivot to put full sunlight on the subject. The celebrated actor, Joseph Jefferson (left), shown in costume for his most popular role, Rip Van Winkle, was a stockholder in the company.

Jefferson invited Dickson and his assistant, Billy Bitzer, to his estate in Massachusetts to film scenes from the play for the company's program.

using films as an interlude in a miscellaneous vaudeville show; and in America a number of entrepreneurs opened storefront theaters, forerunners of nickelodeons. Among these were men like William T. Rock and Thomas Tally, who would subsequently become prominent figures in the burgeoning cinema business.

THE INHERITED REPERTOIRE

Origins of motion picture content

THE FIRST FILMMAKERS DID NOT SUDDENLY INVENT A new form. Rather they relied upon existing patterns and analogies. Only by taking this into account can we comprehend, for instance, the essential difference between the repertoire of the Kinetoscope and the first motion pictures intended for projection.

The clue to the Kinetoscope strategy lies in the term that William Dickson used in registering the first films for copyright, "Edison Kinetoscope records." From the start, the term "records" had been applied to cylinders made on and for the phonograph; and it is clear from Dickson's choice of the word that films were seen as the visual equivalent of phonograph cylinders. The Kinetoscope, as Edison had often said, was "an instrument which could do for the eye what the phonograph does for the ear." Paul Spehr has pointed out the particular significance of the term "record": "I think that for Edison both the Phonograph and the Kinetograph were machines made to record something as a 'permanent' copy of it. The light bulb and telegraph transmitted transitory things. Phonograph and Kinetograph recorded things."

The phonograph, once commercialized, was used to record popular songs and popular singers, hymns, instrumentalists, bands, comedians, whistlers, politicians, and imitators of farmyard noises—any aural effect that was entertaining or novel. In the search for exactly analogous visual sensations, Dickson and his associated entrepreneurs turned to the vaudeville bills on offer at Koster and Bial's Music Hall, and came back with Annabelle the dancer, Madame Bertholdi the contortionist, Sandow the strongman, performing animals and jugglers. Later at Biograph, but in the same spirit,

■ In 1898, W. K. L. Dickson spent four months in Rome to photograph Pope Leo XIII. In this frame from a Mutoscope roll the pope is being ushered into the Vatican garden. Pope Leo XIII was born in 1810, when Napoleon was still Europe's dominant political figure. After the films were accepted by the Vatican and shown to prominent American prelates, they were premiered in New York's Carnegie Hall.

Dickson filmed Pope Leo XIII, five years before the pope permitted his voice to be recorded by Bettini in 1903. Since Pope Leo was born in 1810, he is almost certainly the earliest personality to have been recorded in both sound and image. Dickson's films, which climaxed with the pontiff blessing the Biograph, were premiered at Carnegie Hall.

The Vitascope, Cinématographe, Biograph, and other devices that projected motion pictures on a screen invoked analogies different from the peep show Kinetoscope and consequently a different repertoire. The first projecting mechanisms stood in front of an ordinary magic lantern in the position normally occupied by the glass lantern slide. Many if not most of the first moving picture showmen were lanternists, who regarded this new accessory as an unusually complicated mechanical lantern slide—which in a sense it was. Many film mechanisms were devised so that they could be easily swung from their position in front of the lantern to permit the projection of normal

THE INHERITED REPERTOIRE

still slides. In July 1896 *The Optical Magic Lantern Journal* noted, "If this boom continues, no lanternist's outfit will be complete without a kineto-scopic camera-projector, and no lantern show will be complete without a series of animated pictures." Star lantern lecturers like Lyman Howe easily absorbed films into their stock-in-trade.

It was perfectly natural that *The Optical Magic Lantern Journal* of London should in time become *The Kinematograph and Lantern Weekly*, the world's first regular film journal. The pioneer American magazine for cinema pro-fessionals, *The Moving Picture World*, in its first years also served the stere-opticon trade, and regularly carried articles and advertisements of interest to magic lantern showmen.

Films and lantern slides were listed side by side in the catalogues of established stereopticon dealers like McAllisters or the Kleine Optical Com-pany of Chicago, Briggs or Siegmund Lubin (destined to be a prominent film producer) in Philadelphia, Hughes or Butchers of London, or Riley of Bradford. (The lantern trade was international, as the film trade would become; when Edison required lantern slides in October 1888, McAllisters sent him catalogues of all the European dealers). Films were at first adver-tised, rented, and sold exactly in the same way as lantern slides.

The repertoires were so similar that catalogue descriptions of slides and films are hardly distinguishable. The subject headings in the American Muto-scope and Biograph catalogue, as late as 1902, are precisely those which might have appeared in a lantern slide catalogue: "Comedy, Vaudeville, Trick, Sports and Pastimes, Notable Personages, Railroads, Scenic, Fire and Police, Military, Parades, Marine, Children, Educational, Expositions, Machinery, Miscellaneous." For that matter these headings could as easily have categorized a stock of stereographs or picture postcards—a repertoire still not far removed from that of the lantern and the early cinema.

The first one-shot comedies, too, reveal their origins in static lantern slides. The endless variations on naughty children playing tricks on their elders, of tramps stealing food but being caught, of inebriate husbands returning home to be belabored by their wives, of young men caught kissing girls are all anticipated in the lantern catalogues—often figuring in the pop-ular "catastrophe series" consisting of two-slide, cause-and-effect sets.

Gradually, however, the film revealed its own specificity, possibilities that left the static slide behind. From the start, the dynamic of crashing waves or of trains and fire engines rushing at the audience provided an excitement which lantern slides, though they frequently depicted these same subjects, could not in any way equal.

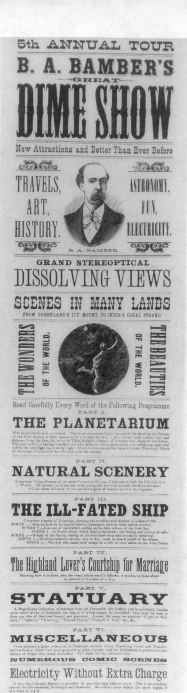

■ The exhibition, sale, and rental of lantern slides was a thriving business, which was a model for the infant movie business. Movie catalogues borrowed classifications such as "Comedy," "Trick," "Sports," "Military," etc., from lantern slide catalogs. Touring magic lantern shows like *B. A. Bamber's Great Dime Show* (left) provided an early market for movies, and movie producers made film versions of subjects shown in lantern programs. Lantern slide dealers, like Chicago's Kleine Optical Company, were early distributors of movies. The Kleine delivery wagon shown in this picture (above right) is carrying projectors for movies and slides (left). Exhibitors using such a combination would show slides while changing the film reels, which rarely ran more than one minute.

In time the excitement of movement for its own sake wore off; but in early 1898, just when the interest of the vaudeville public was visibly waning, film-makers discovered that certain current events could give their shows new excitement and appeal. The mysterious explosion that destroyed the battle-ship *Maine* in Havana harbor on February 15, 1898, roused violent anti-Spanish, pro-Cuban feeling in the United States. Filmmakers responded swiftly to the national emotion. Film of the *Maine*'s sister ships was shame-lessly presented as showing the ill-fated vessel herself. The newly formed Vitagraph Company scored a nationwide triumph with its *Tearing Down the Spanish Flag*, whose total production resources were a flagpole, two 18-inch flags, and a hand that tore down the Spanish flag and replaced it with the Stars and Stripes. With the collaboration of the war-mongering William Randolph Hearst, both Edison and Biograph sent cameramen to Cuba. Edison's man was William F. Paley, while Biograph sent Billy Bitzer and Arthur Marvin. Their films of the troops, the commanders, the ships, the scenery, intimate scenes of camp life, and particularly such incidents as the burial of the *Maine* victims were a huge attraction in the theaters. At the Eden Musée, New York, an ever-changing record of war scenes attracted all the soldiers in town—which was in turn a further attraction for the civilian public.

Other wars provided stirring new subjects. Biograph sent C. Fred Ackerman to the Philippines in 1899–1900 to film U.S. military operations, and to China to record the Boxer Rebellion of 1900. Dickson himself, now based in Europe in charge of Biograph's London office, sailed for South Africa in October 1899 and remained there until July 1900, filming the Boer War and recording his experiences in a book, *The Biograph in Battle*. Other companies were content to stage their "war" scenes at home: Sigmund Lubin, the stereop-ticon dealer turned film producer, cheerfully announced his "counterparts" as "Just Received from the battlefield." This sounds like a deliberate attempt to mislead, but in general audiences were possibly neither deceived nor disap-pointed by reenactments or "counterparts" of battles and boxing matches. There was no precedent for news films, and even photographic illustrations in magazines and newspapers were a very recent innovation. The public was still much more accustomed to "artists' impressions" as illustrations of news events, and movie restagings of actuality were exactly analogous to these.

New technical devices and discoveries also began to distance films from lantern slides. Revolving heads for camera tripods enabled Edison and Bio-graph to add to their catalogues exciting scenic panoramas of subjects like the 1900 Paris Exposition or disasters like the Galveston Flood. More important however were the trick films of Georges Méliès, which began to arrive from

■ The novelty of action captivated early audiences. Ships, railroads, parades, and fire departments were particularly popular subjects. Showmen bought or rented single-subject rolls of film that could be presented as they chose. These three films of the Newark, N.J., fire department, made by Edison in 1897, show a fire department leaving the station (above left) and racing to a fire on two Newark streets (below left and below)—a logical order. They could be shown independently or in sequence. After 1900, film producers began to take control of the way films were structured and viewed. Edwin S. Porter's early classic *The Life of an American Fireman* (Edison, 1903) combined short documentaries of fire departments with staged dramatic footage to create a story about a fire at a fireman's home (facing page, left and right). Scenes are joined in an order chosen by Porter and exhibitors received the film as a single reel.

Paris around the turn of the century. Méliès, a magician turned filmmaker, revealed the cinema's unique and almost limitless possibilities for trickery and special effects through stop action, superimposition, multiple exposure, and a host of other devices that he used with marvelous invention and wit.

Méliès, too, definitively transformed the cinema into a narrative medium. He boasted of his role as inventor of "artificially arranged scenes." Having built a glasshouse studio at Montreuil-sous-Bois, near Paris, he consistently

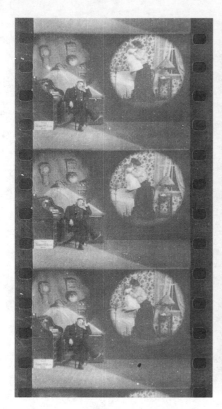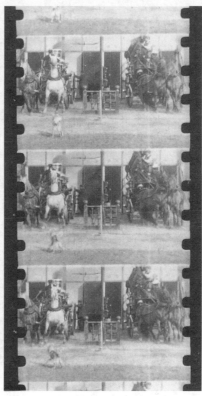

staged his films, with painted scenery and specially designed costumes—
creating his own fantasy universe at a time when most filmmakers were still
content simply to photograph the world as it appeared before them.

Before Méliès, a film was an entity, a single shot complete in itself and
generally running for something less than one minute. An 1899 Biograph
"phantom ride," shot with a camera fixed to the front of a train crossing the
Brooklyn Bridge, demonstrates an early experiment in joining a number of
films together. Several successive, one-minute pieces of film have been skillfully edited together in such a way that the changes and joins are hardly dis-
cernible. This early use of editing serves simply to extend the length of a
film, without attempting to combine disparate and complementary elements.
By 1898 however Méliès was using two or three "films" as scenes in a single
story. Each scene appeared in his catalogue as a separate film, however, and
even when he made an ambitious recreation of the Dreyfus Affair in 1899, it
was marketed as twelve individual films—just as a set of lantern slides might
have been sold under individual titles.

■ Public enthusiasm for the Spanish-American War was exploited by movie makers. Audiences cheered Edison's *Old Glory and Cuban Flag*, a simple tableau in which an American flag is pulled away to reveal the new Cuban flag (above left, right, and facing page, left). Although cameramen were sent to Cuba, the bulky cameras that used short film rolls made combat coverage difficult. Imaginative filmmakers recreated battles in films like *Advance of Kansas Volunteers at Caloocan* (Edison 1899) (facing page, right). Staged reenactments seem deceptive, but in 1899, audiences were not used to seeing authentic news photographs.

The following year the Biograph Company made two moral dramas, *The Downward Path* and *A Career of Crime*, which respectively told the sad stories of a girl and a boy who went to the bad. Again however the five one-minute scenes that made up each story were catalogued separately: the purchaser was not obliged to take all the scenes, or even to show them in any special order.

In 1899 however Méliès for the first time assembled several scenes into a single film, in *Cinderella*. Although still listed in the catalogue under six numbers, the different scenes were linked by dissolves—a device familiar from

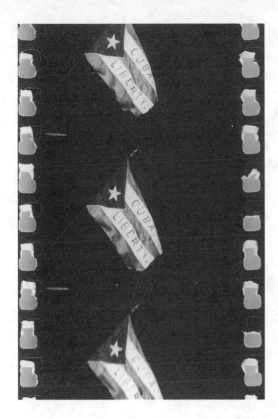

the magic lantern. After this his story films grew progressively more ambitious, as he adapted subjects like *Blue Beard* (1901), *Robinson Crusoe* (1902), *The Damnation of Faust* (1903, inspired by Berlioz), and *Faust and Marguerite* (1904, inspired by Gounod). *The Kingdom of the Fairies* (1903) reached the unprecedented length of 1,080 feet—more than 15 minutes, although his masterpiece and most popular film was the incomparable *A Trip to the Moon* (1902), a witty parody of Jules Verne and H. G. Wells.

Méliès' films were hugely successful in the United States, and in consequence were pirated—even by the Edison Company—and imitated. By the beginning of the century American filmmakers were starting to make two-scene and three-scene films—not in itself a revolutionary move, given that lantern slides had for years been telling stories in series of pictures that might range from four or six in number to thirty or more.

In 1900 the Edison Manufacturing Company resumed a leading role as film producers. Motion picture activities were regenerated, the Black Maria was finally abandoned, and a new roof-top glass-house studio at East 21st

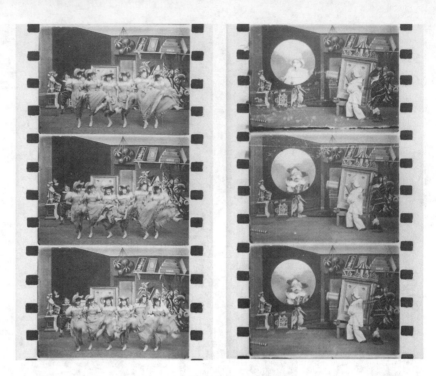

■ The most creative pioneer filmmaker was the Frenchman Georges Méliès. A professional magician and illusionist, Méliès saw the camera as an instrument to enhance his skills. In *The Magic Lantern* (1903) he transforms a crude box into a lantern that mysteriously shows moving images.

■ In 1900, the American Mutoscope Company began to release "series" pictures that told a dramatic story in a sequence of individual scenes. This page from the company's 1902 catalogue promotes the related episodes of *A Career of Crime* for projection or to attract a paying audience to several Mutoscope machines.

THE FATAL WEDDING

MISCELLANEOUS

ALL subjects not properly classified on the foregoing pages will be found here, and among them are many of the "hit" pictures of our list. All animal subjects not featured as vaudeville acts, are included here, as are also a number of dramatic subjects, such as the great "series" pictures, "The Career of Crime", "The Downward Path", "Ten nights in a Bar-Room", etc. The "series" pictures are particularly strong in Mutoscope work, as they serve to hold the attention of a customer through a group of machines. They are no less available for projecting machines, however, for each subject will be found to be a powerful unit in itself.

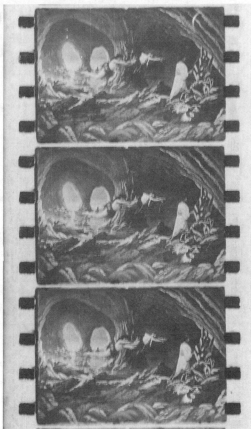

■ Edwin S. Porter was America's most important early filmmaker (left). Originally a cameraman, he became a director but often combined the roles. In 1902, he started making one-reel dramatic films that told stories through linked and related scenes. *Jack and the Beanstalk* (Edison 1902), Porter's first longer story film borrowed both style and structure from France's George Méliès. Frames from two fantasies for children, *Jack and the Beanstalk* (above left) and Méliès' 1903 film *The Fairyland; or, The Kingdom of the Fairies* (above right), show similarities and differences in their styles.

Street was completed in January 1901 at a cost of $2,800. Most important, Edwin S. Porter, who had been involved with the film presentations of the Eden Musée, was hired, initially to improve the technical facilities. In this role his first achievement was to create a new projecting Kinetoscope with a capacity of 1,000 feet. This ability to show longer films (with film speed becoming more or less standardized at around 16 frames per second, the projector was capable of 15 minutes unbroken screening) was to have far-reaching effects upon the development of film production.

Porter, working at first in collaboration with George S. Fleming, an actor and scene painter, was however to transform the technique of the American story film. At the Eden Musée, he may have been involved in the compilation of the 1898 presentation of films and slides called *Panorama of the War*. In 1901 he and Fleming were responsible for *The Execution of Czolgosz with Panorama of Auburn Prison*. This was a collection of four one-shot films, two of them actuality shots of the outside of the prison and two acted reconstructions of the execution of the assassin of President McKinley. The films were sold separately, but the exhibitor was invited to put them together to make a whole narrative. *Jack and the Beanstalk* (1902) was an elaborate production, in direct imitation of the Méliès style, which told its story through a series of ten distinct tableau scenes, still in the manner of a set of lantern slides.

The Life of an American Fireman (1902) also had its origins in lantern slides. The work of the new civic services and the danger to which firemen were exposed was a stirring theme for late nineteenth-century audiences. Numerous lantern series about firemen were succeeded by innumerable one-shot films of fire fighters and fire engines in action. The lantern series dramatized their subject by showing sentimental scenes of individual rescues alongside the more spectacular images. And Porter did precisely this in *The Life of an American Fireman*. Its nine shots put together actuality scenes of firemen and fire engines in action, with dramatized scenes showing an individual fireman dreaming (in a double exposure) of an imperiled woman and child; and a climactic scene in which he enters an upper room to save the self-same woman and child.

The Méliès or magic lantern method of telling a story depended upon a succession of separate tableau scenes. Porter introduced a causal linkage between the shots, which vastly heightened their cumulative dramatic effect. Moreover while Méliès' stories were fantastic, Porter's were contemporary and familiar in setting. The instant response of the audience (not to speak of the plagiarists) clearly convinced Porter that he had discovered a new way of telling stories.*

He developed the method to telling effect the following year with *The Great Train Robbery*, which was to prove the most influential film of the

---

*For American cinema. English filmmakers like Williamson, Mottershaw, Haggar, and G. A. Smith were already using very fluid narrative editing styles by this date, among other films in James Williamson's *Fire!*

THE INHERITED REPERTOIRE

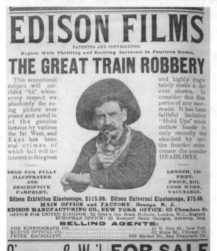

■ *The Great Train Robbery* (Edison 1903), Porter's most famous and influential film (above left), was so popular that it continued to be shown for years after first release. *Moving Picture World* estimated that it had earned $2 million by 1908. Big bucks for its time! The Edison Company recognized its potential and promoted it with a strong campaign of ads like this one that appeared in the *New York Clipper*, December 12, 1903 (left). Rival producers blatantly imitated successful films and Siegmund Lubin released his version of *The Great Train Robbery* in June 1904, six months after Edison's. Shot near Philadelphia with different actors, it duplicates almost every scene in Porter's original (above right).

American cinema's first decade. Much of the lantern slide method still lingers: the film is told in a succession of one-shot scenes; the action is shown in long-shot; in interior scenes the screen is still used like a stage proscenium; to be wholly comprehensible the narrative might still require the help of the lecturer who frequently officiated at film shows at this period, elucidating and embellishing the action according to his histrionic gifts. The scenes however are skillfully linked one to another and the story is told with confidence and vigor. Open air scenes suggest novel compositions to the filmmakers. The theme moreover has no precedent in the lantern repertory. Loosely based on a popular road-show drama of the same name, *The Great Train Robbery* tells a sensational contemporary crime story.

The film proved a tremendous success, confirming the American public's taste for story films, particularly when they were as exciting as this. A stylistic novelty of *The Great Train Robbery* was a close-up of the gangster chief, pointing his gun threateningly at the audience. It had no narrative function and, the printed synopsis advised exhibitors, could be shown either at the beginning or the end of the film: "The resulting excitement is great." An incorrigible plagiarist, Siegmund Lubin copied the film shot by shot, including the close-up, and advertised that this picture "is so realistic that women scream, and even though no sound is heard, they put their fingers in their ears to shut out the noise of the firing."

Two somewhat different categories of film—the prizefight and the Passion play—were to assume individual importance in the repertoire of the early years. From the start, fight films clearly demonstrated that movies could be big business. The Lathams proved the commercial attraction of prizefights with the Leonard–Cushing and Corbett–Courtney contests filmed in the Black Maria. When the Latham group broke up, Enoch Rector and Samuel Tilden Jr. inherited the agreement with James Corbett, and formed the Veriscope Company with the intention of filming a championship match between Corbett and Robert Fitzsimmons. Now however an actual fight, not merely scenes specially staged in a studio, would be filmed.

Rector, an engineer by training, devised a special camera using large format film and a wide lens that could take in the entire ring. The enterprise was fraught with difficulty. Pugilism was prohibited in every state of the union: fighters like Corbett were forced to earn their living in the theater, introducing sparring exhibitions under the guise of stage business. After a number of abortive and costly prior efforts to find a location for the fight, the Nevada legislature was persuaded to legalize prizefighting, and a match was arranged in Carson City on March 17, 1897. Filmed by a relay of several cameras at the same viewpoint, the finished film appears to have run for more than one hour.

The Corbett–Fitzsimmons fight was premiered on May 22 at the New York City Academy of Music, where it was accompanied (when he could be heard above the excitement of the audience) by a commentator who stood beside the screen. Enthusiasm was immense. Paradoxically the forbidden sport could be seen quite legitimately on the screen, and women, who could never attend a live match with propriety, were said to be prominent in the audience. The film was shown throughout the country—business often stimulated by the protests of censorious antipugilism lobbies—and was still getting sporadic bookings at the turn of the century.

Siegmund Lubin launched his career as a plagiarist with a counterfeit version of the Corbett–Fitzsimmons fight, said to have been performed by a

Prizefights were very important to the development of the movies. The Corbett–Fitzsimmons fight, a heavyweight championship fight between James Corbett and challenger Robert Fitzsimmons, was staged in Carson City, Nevada, March 17, 1897, by the Veriscope Company, whose cameras were housed in the shed behind the ring (above). The Veriscope camera used a wide film similar to today's wide screen formats (right). The film premiered in New York May 22, 1897.

couple of freight-handlers from the Pennsylvania Railroad. Lubin's disappointed and often angry audiences at least discovered the meaning of the words "counterpart" and "facsimile."

During the next decade or so boxing and wrestling films challenged film technique and always commanded a big box-office. The climax and the end came with the sensational Jeffries–Johnson match in Reno, Nevada, on July 4, 1910, which was filmed by a consortium of the licensed companies, under

the supervision of J. Stuart Blackton. When the young black fighter Johnson knocked out the veteran white fighter, wrote Terry Ramsaye, "he also terminated the prizefight picture for the United States." Racial resentment found expression in a sudden upsurge of moral condemnation of prizefight pictures and nationwide efforts to ban the film on the pretext that it might incite race riots. Two years later the Sims bill made it illegal to transport any motion picture of a fight across state borders—a curious parallel of the Mann Act, which coincidentally was provoked by Jack Johnson's marriage to a white woman, Lucille Cameron.

THE INHERITED REPERTOIRE

■ Four cameras of the American Mutoscope and Biograph Company are ready to film the Jeffries–Sharkey fight in the Coney Island Sporting Club, November 3, 1899 (facing page). The camera operators are (left to right) Frederick S. Armitage, Billy Bitzer (with mustache), Arthur Marvin, and Wallace McCutcheon. Harry Marvin is standing in the middle of the cameras. The others are unidentified. A decade later, in 1910, the victory of Jack Johnson (left) over the former white champion, Jim Jeffries, stimulated antiboxing legislation that ended the profitable business of filming boxing matches.

Passion play films had firm roots in the magic lantern repertoire. Religious organizations were among the best customers for lantern slides in the 1890s. An extensive series of slides on the life of Christ after the painter Tissot remained for many years in the catalogues, as did slides illustrating successive productions of the decennial Oberammergau Passion play.

The 1880 and 1890 Oberammergau performances had attracted considerable attention in the United States, thanks to the illustrated press and increasing European tourism. In 1896 the Lumières' American representative, Charles Smith Hurd, negotiated a contract to film a less-publicized Passion play that had been performed in the Austrian village of Horitz since 1816. Financial backing for the project came from the theatrical producers Marc Klaw and Abraham J. Erlanger. The filmed scenes, interspersed with lantern slides, and accompanied by music and a lecturer, were exhibited with great success in Philadelphia and Boston.

By the time the show reached New York, however, as a special Lenten presentation at Daly's Theater, a rival version was already playing at the Eden Musée on 23d Street. Irked at not getting the Horitz contract with Hurd, Richard Hollaman, proprietor of the Musée—a characteristic nineteenth-century institution purveying a mixture of amusement and instruction for the middle classes—had determined to make his own Passion play. He rented

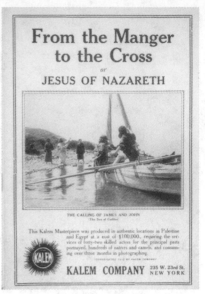

■ Religious subjects were also important to the development of the movies. The October 22, 1898, issue of *The New York Clipper* has two ads for versions of the Passion play (above left). The version by the Eden Musée claims authenticity, protection by copyright and by Edison's patents. Siegmund Lubin offers a two-hour version with slides and a lecture. The Kalem Company's *From the Manger to the Cross,* made in 1912, was the best and most enduring American version of the life of Christ (above right). Sidney Olcott directed a company of American and English actors on locations in Egypt and Palestine. The script was by actress-writer Gene Gauntier, who also played Mary. Sunday-school classes and church groups saw versions of this film for many years after theater showings ended.

some costumes made almost thirty years before for a theatrical Passion play devised by Salmi Morse that had been aborted as a result of religious protests. The filming was done on the roof of the Grand Central Palace. A stage producer, Henry Vincent, was called in to supervise, paint the scenery, and direct the actors. (According to Terry Ramsaye, Vincent labored under the delusion that he was photographing lantern slides, and stopped the action whenever a desirable composition was achieved.) Although Hollaman modified his original claim that the film showed the actual Oberammergau Passion play, the production won the approval of church spokesmen and hence the profitable patronage of their flocks.

The twenty-three separate films that constituted the Passion play could be bought individually or in sets of varying number; and individual showmen were free to devise their own presentations, using lantern slides, lecturers, and suitable music. McAllister's 1900 catalogue lists fifty lantern slides along with the films (which by this time had passed to Edison), noting, "In connection with the above [slides] we would suggest the following Edison Films, which could be appropriately interspersed with the above set of lantern slides."

The first Passion plays were followed by others. Several versions were imported from France—the best two made by the Pathé Company. Every company felt obliged to offer its own Passion play; and in later years it is often difficult to know which of the many versions is being advertised, for instance by Siegmund Lubin, who accompanied his with an elaborate booklet including a lecture and directions for a two-hour presentation. The last and greatest Passion play of the period, Kalem's *From the Manger to the Cross*, filmed in the Holy Land, arrived in late 1912.

The demand for Passion plays, especially during Lent, remained high; exhibitors who had failed to secure a copy of one would insert desperate pleas in the trade press. The plays continued to merit special presentations, with lecturers and interpolated slides; and the *Moving Picture World*'s W. Stephen Bush, a star lecturer, regularly advertised his services to present them.

FINDING A HOME

*The rise of the nickelodeon and the
purpose-built cinema*

THE COMING OF THE STORY FILM TRANSFORMED MOTION
pictures from yesterday's faded novelty to the nation's universal pastime. By
the opening of the century, with no more wars to enliven the repertoire, moving picture turns had again lost favor with the vaudeville theaters, who either
ceased booking them altogether, or relegated them to the position of
"chaser" on the bill—the unattractive act that helped the audience decide to
leave a nonstop show. The new story films however set managements wooing picture showmen all over again.

Meanwhile, storefront theaters, which had never before been able to compete with the vaudeville presentations, began to boom. The old mixed programs of one-minute travel films and one-point gags were acceptable as a short
turn in a large variety bill. Exciting stories like *A Trip to the Moon*, *The Great
Train Robbery*, or *A Bold Bank Robbery* merited a showplace of their own.

The official birthplace of the nickelodeon was Pittsburgh. Harry Davis, a
vaudeville impresario and real-estate speculator (the combination is significant) recognized the attraction of films in his vaudeville houses, and in 1904
opened a small room with four-minute film projections in the rear of a penny
arcade. When the arcade burnt down he converted a store on Smithfield
Street into a cinema theater, which he opened in June 1905 and named the
Nickelodeon. The name was not new for 5-cent shows of one sort or another;
but it was now definitively adopted to designate this kind of show and this
era of the cinema industry.

Davis' Nickelodeon was, reported a Pittsburgh newspaper, "the first theater in America devoted to moving pictures exclusively. The first show was

in the nature of an experiment, without music, song or other accompaniments, and the presentation consisted of only 500 feet of film. The people of Pittsburgh came and saw, and capitulated." Within two months the Nickelodeon had proved so successful that Davis spent $7,000 on a new frontage. Within two years he had opened fifteen theaters in various cities.

From the start Davis set high standards. His theaters stayed open for fifteen and a half hours a day but, unlike many other shows, his employees worked only eight-hour shifts. "Each employee is furnished with a tasteful uniform, made in the firm's own tailoring establishment in Pittsburgh."

This, said the same Pittsburgh newspaper, "was the origin of the movement which has spread to all corners of the civilized globe." Within a year there were forty-two theaters in Pittsburgh, and nickelodeons were spreading like wildfire across the states, with names like Nickolette, Dreamland, Theatorium, Pictorium, Jewel, Electric (naturally), Majestic (which they often were not) and Bijou Dream, which was Davis' own favorite.

"An army of perhaps forty thousand keen, money-hungry human beings were engaged in a mad-house scramble to acquire fortunes through this fascinating new business of selling cheap entertainment," wrote Benjamin B. Hampton in his *History of the American Film Industry*. By the autumn of 1906 New York was reckoned to have more nickel theaters than any other city in the United States (which meant in the world), and new theaters were still opening daily. Figures are hard to assess but Eileen Bowser has gathered available statistics, which suggest that the number of nickelodeons in the United States doubled between 1907 and 1908 to around 8,000, and by 1914, when the 5c theater was already being supplanted by grander houses, was around 14,000. By 1910 it was estimated that 26 million Americans visited these theaters every week.

It is a mistake to imagine uniformity among the theaters. True, very many were small stores, hastily converted with 99 or fewer kitchen chairs; in some states this limitation on seating was the necessary qualification for exemption from a costly theater license. Others however were halls that might seat several hundred people. Nor were the nickelodeon owners all small-time impresarios. Some, certainly, were clever young Jewish immigrants like Adolph Zukor, Carl Laemmle, and the brothers Warner who invested their small savings in theaters as the first step on the road to becoming the makers of the American film industry. At the other end of the scale however the important B. F. Keith vaudeville circuit either temporarily or permanently converted out-of-season or unprofitable live theaters into nickelodeons, some with capacities for well over one thousand viewers.

■ "...a new thing under the sun—" A new industry trade paper, *The Moving Picture World*, extols the potential of the nickelodeon. Storefront theaters showing movies continuously are "multiplying faster than guinea pigs," "all you have to do is open the doors, start the phonograph, and carry the money to the bank." The nickelodeon was anticipated by the short-lived Vitascope Theater, which opened June 28, 1896, in New Orleans. Its 20-minute program of Edison films was probably the first exclusive showing of moving pictures. The proprietors were Walter Wainwright (right) and William T. "Pop" Rock (left). Later Rock became a partner in the Vitagraph Company.

Exhibition practices were as variable. Programs ranged between 10 minutes and half an hour or more in length. Generally they ran continuously (like many vaudeville programs), but in other theaters there was a pause between shows for a change of reels and a change of audience. Opening hours were conditioned by the locale, and the number of shows could range from fewer than twenty to more than forty in a day.

The nickelodeon show might mix with the films any suitable or affordable combination of vaudeville acts and singers, accompanied by lantern slides illustrative of their songs. In theaters with only one projector, the singer was useful to cover the reel changes. Some theaters were designed with a niche beside the stage in which the singer would perform, and this

■ "Loud Talking or Whistling Not Allowed." Enterprising nickelodeon owners welcomed their audiences with lantern slides. Most nickelodeons had only one projector so slides diverted the audience while reels were being changed, when there was a mechanical problem or a broken film. Slides also gave droll messages about proper behavior (see chapter openings).

might alternatively accommodate the "lecturer" who lingered on in many places until the 'teens and the arrival of the multireel feature. Before intertitles became a regular convention, the lecturer was useful to elucidate the screen story: synopses issued to advertise the films frequently indicate much in the story that is far from obvious in the pictures themselves. Lecturers were often local stars in their own right.

The musical provision was variable: "The enterprising manager usually engages a human pianist with instructions to play Eliza-crossing-the-ice when the scene is shuddery, and fast ragtime in a comic kid chase. When there is little competition, however, the manager merely presses a button and starts the automatic going, which is just as likely to bellow out, 'I'd rather two-step than waltz, Bill,' just as the angel rises from the brave little hero-cripple's corpse" (*Moving Picture World*).

The popular memory of the nickelodeon as a riotous, noisome place, with an out-of-tune piano and odors of flesh and food, however, is misleading. Russell Merritt has demonstrated ("Nickelodeon Theaters 1905–1914") that while some might degenerate into dormitories for transients, others determinedly aimed to attract a middle-class family audience. The nickelodeons tended to reflect the social aspirations of their upward-striving proprietors.

The all-day operation of many shows and the brevity of the performance brought a new kind of theater-going. Workers could drop in to see a show in their lunch break and housewives could take a rest from their marketing or shopping. The nickelodeon was unprecedented as a wholly democratic entertainment. The low price was accessible to almost anyone and the uniform price of seats eliminated the economic (though often not the racial) discrimination characteristic of even the most modest vaudeville houses.

In January 1908 *The Moving Picture World* reported that:

> the character of the attendance varies with the locality, but whatever the locality, children make up about thirty-three per cent of the crowds. For some reason, young women from sixteen to thirty years old are rarely in evidence, but many middle-aged and old women are steady patrons, who never, when a new film is to be shown, miss the opening.
>
> In cosmopolitan city districts, the foreigners attend in larger proportion than the English-speakers. This is doubtless because the foreigners, shut out as they are by their alien tongues from much of the life about them, can yet perfectly understand the pantomime of the moving pictures.

The immigrant audiences nevertheless shared enthusiasm for this uniquely accessible entertainment with their native fellows. Even if some middle-class, puritan, and religious groups would remain suspicious of moving pictures unless they were presented in churches or by educational lecturers like Lyman Howe, many other white-collar groups found themselves attracted. Showmen made a conscious appeal to women and children. Most of the shows were prominently advertised as "Refined and pleasing to ladies." Children, who often made up the larger part of the audiences, were often segregated, not in those days for their own safety, but rather for the peace of the adults.

A vivid picture of the nickelodeon audience and middle-class attitudes is provided by a woman correspondent of the *Boston Journal* writing in May 1909. She says that most of her acquaintances have acquired the moving picture habit, "though for some reason they one and all seem loath to acknowledge the fact." While waiting in the entrance of a nickelodeon for a woman friend with whom she had shared the secret of her own addiction, she observed the people who entered, some of them known to her—men and women, single or in groups; a bank official, a family party, a woman store clerk, women shoppers, businessmen, a doctor, the butcher.

> "Beside those whom I recognized or had some inkling of their object in life, there were twenty others as interesting and as different in appearance as those I have described.
>
> "I was about to give my friend up and venture in alone when another figure loomed before me which made me feel quite conscious. It was

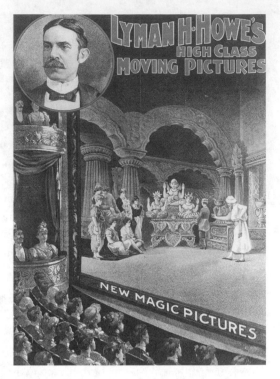

■ "Lyman H. Howe's High Class Moving Pictures." An experienced lanternist and educational lecturer, Lyman Howe toured the country presenting programs of moving pictures suitable for middle-class audiences, particularly women and children.

that of a woman friend of mine who seemed to shrink within herself when she saw me. She felt as I felt no doubt—like a child caught at the jam pot. We smilingly exchanged greetings, she murmured something about 'enjoying them so much,' to which I promptly responded, 'So do I.' The friend whom I had been expecting pushed me through the door . . . and we gave ourselves up to the enjoyment of an entertainment that appeals to all sorts, rich and poor, intelligent and unintelligent, which is instructive and helpful as well as amusing."

This woman echoed the optimism of many enlightened educators and reformers about the potential of "the people's theater." Few people, noted *The Moving Picture World* (May 4, 1907), "realize the important part these theaters are beginning to play in city life. They have been looked upon largely as places of trivial amusement, not calling for any serious consideration. They seem, however, to be something that may become one of the greatest forces for good or for evil in the city."

An off-shoot of the nickelodeon era was an entertainment presented by the former Kansas City fire chief George C. Hale. "Hale's Tours" consisted of a small theater arranged and decorated to appear like the interior of a railway carriage. At one end, as if through the window of an observation car, the audience watched back-projected films of panoramic train rides. Hale's set-up, more elaborate than most of the various imitations that inevitably followed, included machinery to simulate the movement of the carriage. The idea was far from new—it was anticipated by nineteenth-century entertainments involving long panoramas moving between rollers,* among which the Nautical Maréorama at the Paris Exposition of 1900 was one of the most elaborate. Hale exploited his shows with great flair for several years, and successfully opened up an overseas market, with shows in London and Paris.

The more often the program changed, the more often the audience came back. "A year ago and even less," reported *Views and Film Index* in December 1907, "two changes a week in motion picture programs was considered fair and three changes considered good. Today it would be hard to find a nickelodeon in the country that is not furnishing a change of program every day. In some instances . . . two changes a day are offered—one in the afternoon and one in the evening."

The nickelodeons' demand for films was phenomenal and highly competitive, with every exhibitor eager for exclusive first runs. In the first years of the cinema, when the device was still a novelty in itself, showmen had simply bought their films outright from the manufacturers. The new demand for ever-changing shows made this kind of outright purchase impractical, and renting through film exchanges became the general practice. Since the beginning of the century exhibitors had informally exchanged films among themselves, and from 1903 an organized system of "film exchanges" began to evolve. The first recorded regular film exchange was opened that year by Harry and Herbert Miles of San Francisco. The exchanges mushroomed in proportion to the nickelodeons themselves, and by 1907 between 125 and 150 such businesses were in operation.

In the first nickelodeon years Chicago, the traditional industrial distribution center of the midwest, was reckoned to account for 80 percent of the national exchange business. The most significant Chicago exchange owners were George K. Spoor, Eugene Cline, William H. Swanson, and the colorful Carl Laemmle. In New York the theater proprietor William Fox, with his

*Max Ophuls charmingly recreates such a show in his film *Letter from an Unknown Woman* (1948).

■ One of the enterprising immigrants attracted to the movie business by the nickelodeon boom was Carl Laemmle (standing). He posed for this photograph with his friend Theodore Rogestein, shortly after his arrival in Chicago from Germany in 1884. (The photo was marked for cropping in an earlier publication.) In 1906, Laemmle opened a nickelodeon in Chicago. By 1909, he owned film exchanges in several cities and his own film production company. In 1912, he became an officer of the new Universal Film Manufacturing Company, and by 1914 Laemmle controlled the company.

Greater New York Film Rental Company, opened in March 1907, and Marcus Loew moved into the exchange business, as did the Warner Brothers and Harry Davis himself in Pittsburgh.

Given the great demand for films, exhibitors were wholly dependent on the exchanges for the regular supply of ready-made programs. Only the very lucky ones knew in advance what films would arrive on the day; others counted themselves fortunate merely to have films in good enough condition to screen.

With programs changing every day, the demand for new films was insatiable. Domestic production was unable to respond adequately to the demand and the opportunity. Edison had from the start initiated a policy of pursuing unrelentingly anything that could be interpreted as infringement of his patents on apparatus, thereby handicapping rivals and discouraging new entrepreneurs from investing in production. The original pre-1900 companies—Edison, Biograph, Vitagraph, Lubin, and Selig Polyscope—were unable to expand their operations fast enough; and in May 1907 *The Moving Picture World* reported that "the plays that are put on at the 5-cent theaters are for the most part manufactured abroad. Paris is a great producing center. London has numerous factories that grind them out." It was estimated that two-thirds of the films shown in the United States were imported.

■ Movie studios appeared in strange places. This converted store in Bayonne, N.J. housed David Horsley's Centaur Film Company. established in 1908 (above). The photo was autographed by David Horsley's brother, William, to Gerald Badgley, a technician who worked for Centaur. Alice Guy Blaché (right), who began directing films in France in 1896, came to the United States in 1908 with her new husband, Herbert Blaché. In 1911, they founded the Solax Company. Mme Blaché was president and business manager. She managed construction of a new studio, supervised production, wrote scripts, and directed films.

The nickelodeon boom however inevitably stimulated the rise of new production concerns, prepared to risk the Edison threat for the huge profits that lay in wait. The most durable of the companies established in 1907 were Kalem (named from the surname initials of its founders, George Kleine, Samuel Long, and Francis J. Marion) and Essanay (similarly named from its partners George K. Spoor and G. M. Anderson). At first based in New York, Kalem became the most peripatetic of companies, filming in New Jersey, California, Jacksonville, Florida, Ireland, and the Holy Land.

New Jersey became a center of film activity. In 1908 David Horsley established the Centaur Company (later Nestor) in Bayonne, to produce "westerns." In 1910 Mark Dintenfass' Champion Film Company and the French-based Pathé Company built studios in New Jersey. Pathé was the start of a French invasion. In 1911 studios were built in Fort Lee by the French Eclair Company and by a new production house, Solax. The founders of Solax were Alice Guy Blaché, who had become the world's first woman director at Gaumont's Paris studios at the turn of the century, and her husband, Herbert Blaché, manager of Gaumont's American production branch. Another Fort Lee company, Victor, was established in 1912 by Florence Lawrence, then at the height of her fame as one of America's first stars.

The nickelodeon boom brought side effects that were to have far-reaching effects on cinema organization in the United States. The rapid and haphazard development of thousands of theaters, many in buildings ill-adapted to their new use, was full of perils. Nitrate film was notoriously flammable, and fires in cinemas in the years 1905–1907 probably numbered thousands, although the trade press was at pains to underplay the dangers. Many of these fires were small and restricted to the projection box: it was indeed miraculous that there were not more big and fatal conflagrations. However they were sufficient to attract the attention of the police and local authorities and to cause the introduction of regulations which in some places were sensible, in other localities unreasonably onerous.

Fire was only one of the dangers to which operators were exposed, working often twelve hours a day, practically without relief, in hot, oppressive boxes with dangerous and potentially lethal fumes, carbon, and asbestos dust. The demand for operators was so great and the work of handcranking films for twelve hours a day so monotonous that unskilled and juvenile staff were employed, at sweat-shop rates. By 1907 there was already vigorous activity to form unions and demand minimum rates in order to deter proprietors from hiring low-caliber staff. Such moves no doubt had the support of the film exchanges, the life of whose prints could be very considerably shortened by unskilled handling.

■ In the nineteenth century, audiences became acquainted with exotic cultures
through magic lantern shows. This fanciful view of China might have been accompanied by a lecture. During the second half of the century, projected photographs
presented more realistic images of exotic locales.

■ The Thaumatrope is a parlor amusement developed from scientific demonstrations of persistence of vision, the optical characteristic that makes moving pictures possible. When the disk is revolved by means of the threads at the sides, images printed on either side of the disc merge together. The barber (above) will groom the customer's hair (below).

ROLEY POLEY.

■ The Zoetrope uses illustrations drawn on strips of paper to create illusions of motion. The strips are placed inside of a drum and viewed through slits in the side as it revolves. Zoetrope strips can be changed and several viewers can watch at the same time.

■ A poster by Jules Cheret for Théatre Optique, which Emile Reynaud operated in Paris from 1892 until 1900. The theater presented animated stories illustrated by a series of images painted on glass, joined together in a flexible strip and projected.

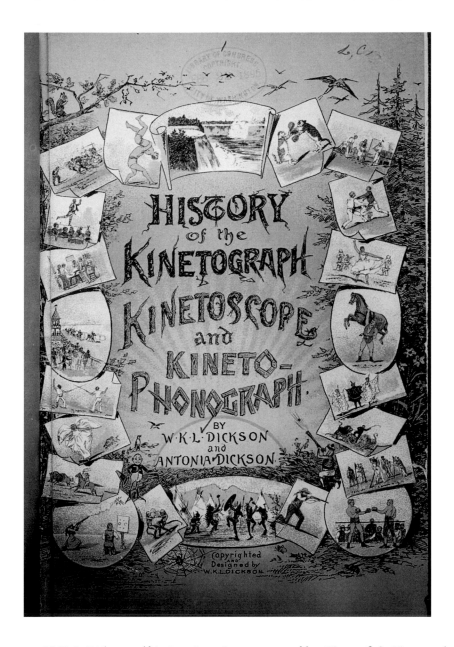

■ W. K. L. Dickson and his sister Antonia wrote a pamphlet, *History of the Kinetograph, Kinetoscope, and Kineto-Phonograph*, which was published in 1895 by Edison's concessionaire, Raff and Gammon, to promote sales of the Kinetoscope. The design and art work for the title page are by W. K. L. Dickson, who surrounded the title with scenes from Kinetoscope films. Some of the films that can be identified are: Corbett-Courtney in the lower right-hand corner; Buffalo Bill to Corbett's left; Annie Oakley in the lower left-hand corner; and Annabelle is the second image above her.

■ The Lumières introduced the Cinematographe to the Parisian public, December 28, 1895, in the basement of the Grand Cafe, Boulevard des Capucines. It captured the public's fancy as no other early motion picture device and France was soon the leader of a growing international market.

■ "Edison's greatest marvel," the Vitascope, premiered at Koster and Bial's Music Hall, 34th Street, New York City, April 23, 1896. Moving pictures were a featured attraction, but shared top billing with dancer Ida Fuller (Loie Fuller's sister) and singer Albert Chevalier. Other variety acts completed the program. This poster features a fanciful portrayal of the Gaiety Girls on its screen. Macy's department store now occupies the site of Koster and Bial's Music Hall.

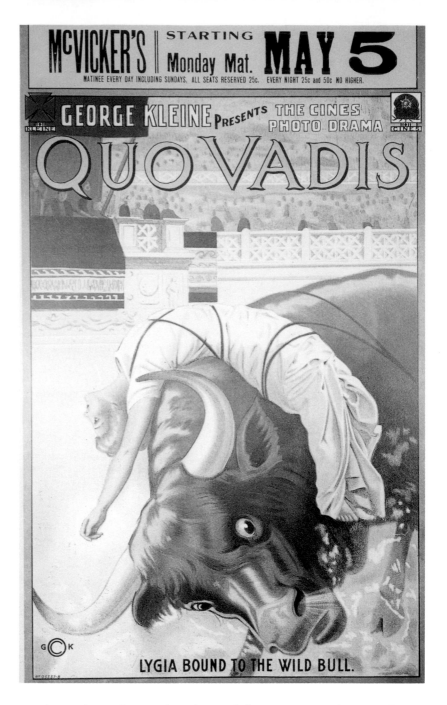

MCVICKER'S | STARTING Monday Mat. MAY 5
MATINEE EVERY DAY INCLUDING SUNDAYS, ALL SEATS RESERVED 25c. EVERY NIGHT 25c and 50c NO HIGHER.

GEORGE KLEINE PRESENTS THE CINES PHOTO DRAMA

QUO VADIS

LYGIA BOUND TO THE WILD BULL.

■ The popularity of spectacular Italian-made features encouraged George Kleine to invest more than $200,000 to import *Quo Vadis* (Cines 1913). The eight-reel Italian spectacle claimed to employ more than 3,500 actors and 40 lions. Kleine made a profit!

Universal City, "The Home of-the Movies," Los Angeles, California—C1

■   As the industry grew, studios grew larger and more sophisticated. Carl Laemmle's Universal City, opened in 1915, was a studio complex that spread over several acres. The curious public could take a tour of the facilities and buy postcards like this to remember the occasion.

■ Audiences often saw movies in a variety of colors and tones, even though raw film was usually black and white. A hand-painted film of Annabelle dancing, much like these two frames from *Annabelle, Fire Dance*, was on the program of the first Vitascope showing in 1896. The changing colors emulate colored gels that were used in Annabelle's stage performances.

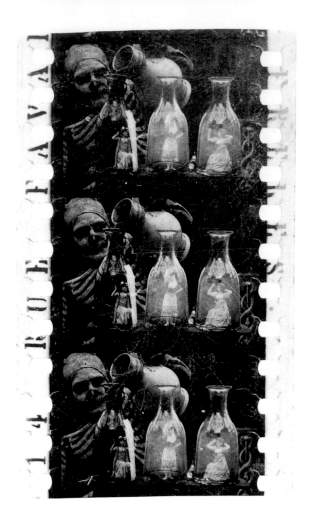

■ Pathé introduced a stencil process that improved color tones for longer films. This is a stencil-colored scene from Pathé's 1907 release *The Red Specter*.

■ The most common way to add color for visual and emotional effects was tinting. Night scenes like this one, from an unidentified Vitagraph film, were photographed during the day and the film was dyed blue to create a more realistic effect. Daylight scenes would be tinted sepia or yellow, emotional scenes might be tinted red, romantic scenes tinted rose, etc.

■ George C. Hale, a former fire chief, created one of the most imaginative movie presentations, Hale's Tours. Hale modified small theaters to simulate a railroad car complete with a rocking motion. Panoramic scenes of train trips were projected on the observation window at the end of the car. The show visited many cities; this colorful postcard is from London.

■ Until World War I, the French firm Pathé Frères was the world's largest producer. Hand-colored fantasy trick films like *The Golden Beetle* (*Le Scarbe d'Or*) (Pathé Freres, 1907) were popular with American audiences.

■ Illustrated posters were issued for almost every film released after 1910. Posters and stills at theater entrances lured customers inside and coordinated ads appeared in newspapers. This colorful poster promotes Selig's *The Moving Picture Cowboy*, a gentle spoof of western films. Its popular star, Tom Mix, was a skilled roper and trick rider.

Lloyds

MISS R BAUL

40-47-80 78463279

OCTOBER BOOKS
SOUTHAMPTON
942 5 N 356 0

1802 1867 2

PLEASE KEEP THIS COPY FOR YOUR RECO

CONFIRMED CARDHOLDER'S SIGNATURE   AUTHORISATIO

Rebecca Baul

CARDHOLDER'S DECLARATION: The issuer of the card identified on this
pay the amount shown as TOTAL upon proper presentation. I p
TOTAL (together with any other charges due thereon) subject to and
with the agreement governing the use of such card.

VISA

DATE
5 2 09

MasterCard
EUROCARD

WARS AND ORDER

Patents wrangles and industrial organization

THE EARLY YEARS OF THE AMERICAN FILM PRODUCTION industry were harassed by the legal activities of the Edison organization. From the moment in August 1897 that the last of the three Edison motion picture patents was issued, the company's lawyers embarked on a sustained campaign to use them as a weapon to eliminate competition. Infringement suits were brought against other manufacturers of equipment and films and even against Edison's own associates, Maguire and Baucus, for selling Lumière and International films as well as Edison's. The campaign continued into the new century. Lubin, Selig, Vitagraph, and Essanay in turn found their resources drained by the cost of litigation. Even though Edison suffered a temporary setback in March 1902, when an appeals court reversed a judgment against the American Mutoscope and Biograph Company, the constant specter of Edison infringement suits remained a critical deterrent to other entrepreneurs in the years up to 1907.

In that year most of the major manufacturers were ready to sue for peace by acknowledging Edison's patent rights. The United Film Services Protection Association, formed to this end in November 1907, foundered, but was succeeded in February 1908 by the Film Service Association, which united Edison and seven licensee-manufacturers—Pathé, Vitagraph, Selig, Lubin, Kalem, Essanay, and Georges Méliès. The American Mutoscope and Biograph Company, having refused to join except on terms of parity with Edison, now cunningly strengthened its bargaining position. The patent on the "Latham loop" (see page 55) having passed to the Ansco Company, Biograph purchased it at auction. Having also signed an agreement with

Armat's company, Biograph was now able to turn the tables on Edison and threaten suit for infringement.

The Edison group eventually capitulated on the terms demanded, and Biograph joined the newly formed Motion Picture Patents Company, which began operation on January 1, 1909. The MPPC, as holding company, proceeded to exploit the various motion picture patents owned by Edison, Biograph, Vitagraph, and Armat, by granting licenses to producers, exchanges, and exhibitors, in consideration for royalty payments. The Trust (as the MPPC was generally known) in addition secured an agreement from the Eastman Company that raw film stock would in future be supplied only to the licensed companies. By this means the Trust set out to secure total monopoly of the motion picture industry at all levels. Determined to restrain new competition, the Trust refused to allow other producers (with the single exception of Kinemacolor, which it admitted in 1913) to join the original licensees. This was to prove a significant miscalculation, serving as it did to create and consolidate supporters for an organized opposition.

This pooling of patent rights to gain monopolistic control was neither new nor viewed as sinister in terms of the industrial politics of the time. The electrical, oil, telephone, and agricultural machinery industries had all witnessed similar strategies.

A central aim of the Trust was to standardize the industry. The manufacturer licensees were committed to produce a certain quota of films, to be released on certain fixed days of each week. Exchanges rented their programs by standing order and paid a standard price, regardless of quality. There was less control of the way that the exchanges served the nickelodeons which, according to the price they paid, might demand brand new films for exclusive first runs, or be satisfied with worn and scratched prints making their last outing before final scrapping.

The Trust from the start was aggressive in enforcing its conditions. Licensed renters and exhibitors frequently complained of oppressive regulation and precipitate cancellation of licenses when regulations were not strictly observed. A whole body of legend grew up about the ferocity with which the Trust pursued the stand-out Independents. Stories of strong-arm men and physical assaults may have been exaggerated; but the reports of Al McCoy, the Trust's private detective, show that there was a zealous espionage system. The sunny picture of the Trust, its officers, its operation, and its critics presented by *The Moving Picture World* in July 1909 does not altogether carry conviction:

■ The Motion Picture Patents Company, created in December 1908, ended the "patent wars," which had kept the industry in turmoil for a decade (right). Discontent against the major producers was particularly intense in Chicago. In March 1908, producer George Spoor of Essanay and William Selig sent Edison's William Gilmore this telegram warning about local dissatisfaction (below right). The industry's corporate powers were filmed at the peace ceremony by the Biograph Company's Billy Bitzer (below left). Left to right: Samuel Long (Kalem Co.), Thomas A. Edison (shaking hands), Edison's attorney Frank Dyer (behind Edison), Jacques Berst (Pathé), George Kleine (Kleine Co., shaking hands with Edison), unidentified head, Frank Marion (Kalem Co.), Albert Smith (Vitagraph Co.), unidentified head, J. Stuart Blackton (Vitagraph Co.).

No new enterprise was ever conceived in this world without provoking opposition. . . . They have been called all sorts of names, which, to the credit of Mr. Dyer, Mr. Kennedy, and their associates, have been borne with cheerful equanimity; they have been accused of depleting the pockets of the unfortunate exhibitor, who, however, in most cases is perfectly well able to take care of his own interests. They have come in for a share of that kind of gentle abuse and criticism which is the peculiar privilege of Mr. Rockefeller, Mr. Harriman, Mr. J. J. Hill, and other successful business men to attract, but, as we have said, all this has been borne with delightful equanimity.

The companies left outside the Trust were not long in banding together. Formed on January 11, 1909, ten days after the Trust itself, the Independent Film Renters Protective Association became the National Independent Moving Picture Alliance in September 1909. One of its first ruses was to launch the Bianchi camera, whose design, with continuously running film, evaded the Edison patents. Since it apparently did not work very well, the Bianchi probably mostly served as a cover while filmmakers were actually using patent cameras.

By autumn 1909 the Alliance had arranged for the supply of Lumière raw film stock from France. The Trust retaliated by urging licensees to use a new Eastman nonflammable film, and endeavoring to persuade civic authorities that ordinary nitrate stock was dangerous and should be prohibited. In turn Lumière also came up with a nonflammable film. When both kinds proved equally unsatisfactory, the Trust had the embarrassing task of going back to the fire departments to convince them that the original nitrate film was quite safe after all.

Encouraged by the Alliance, many new small companies sprang up. As time went on, however, the most influential of the Independents were to be the Great Northern Film Company (importers of the films of the Danish Nordisk Company), the New York Motion Picture Company, Centaur, the Powers Company, Thanhouser, American, Solax and Carl Laemmle.

Laemmle, an exchange owner, had initially been a Trust licensee. After three months however he defected, declaring, "The Motion Picture Patents Company promised to elevate the business, promising to give protection to the little fellow in the small town. They promised everything on earth to make things better, and what have they done? Nothing. Is that right?" Thereafter he became the Trust's most implacable opponent. With the help of an advertising agent, Robert Cochrane, Laemmle embarked on an inspired advertising campaign, ridiculing the Trust with vicious cartoons in the trade press week after week.

Spurred on to set up his own production company, Laemmle offered a $25 prize for the best name, and gave it to a reader of *The Moving Picture World* who came up with the title of Independent Moving Picture Company, with its appropriate acronym IMP.

In 1910 the Laemmle cartoons introduced a new character, General Flimco, to deride a new organization, the General Film Company, set up to take over all the licensed exchanges. Although nominally independent of the

■ Carl Laemmle, a leader of the "independents" resisting the Patents Company (also known as the "Trust"), hired Robert Cochrane, an experienced advertising man to organize a campaign against the Trust. A series of satirical cartoons in the trade press portrayed the Trust as a bloated capitalist exploiting exhibitors (above left). In 1910, Laemmle conducted a contest for a name for his new film company, the Independent Motion Picture Company. Contracted to "IMP", an appropriate cartoon character was also created to bedevil the hated Trust (right).

Trust, the General Film Company's links with it were evident—if only because both organizations were run by the same people. By the end of 1911, General Film had swallowed up every licensed film exchange except William Fox's Greater New York Film Exchange. When Fox would not agree on price with General Film, his license was canceled, and contracted film shipments were refused. Fox instituted litigation that was to contribute to the ultimate downfall of the Trust and its allies.

Meanwhile the Independents had endeavored to set up a comparable centralized exchange organization, the Sales Company, which was itself accused of violating the Sherman Antitrust Act. Subsequently internal dissensions caused the Sales Company to splinter, dividing the Independents into three groups and releasing their films respectively through the Mutual, Universal, and smaller Film Supply organizations.

By 1912 the tide was beginning to turn against the Trust. The Eastman agreement had ended in 1911. The Latham loop patent was overthrown in a suit brought against IMP. William Fox's action charging restraint of trade, although finally settled out of court, undoubtedly spurred the government to bring a suit under the Sherman Antitrust Act. On August 15, 1912, petition was filed in the case of *United States v. Motion Picture Patents Company*. The mass of evidence submitted in the course of a long trial is an invaluable record of early motion picture history. The lower court handed down its decision on October 1, 1915, ruling that "the agreements and acts of the defendants in the present case went far beyond what was necessary to protect the use of the patents or the monopoly which went with them, and that the end and result . . . was the restraint of trade condemned by the law." A decree filed on January 24, 1916, enjoined the defendants and their officers from continuing their unlawful combination. The Motion Picture Patents Company's final appeal in 1918 was dismissed.

Even by the time the case came to court however the demise of the Trust was inevitable. The strength of the Independents' opposition was insuperable. The process of litigation on which the Trust relied was of its nature financially exhausting, and the Trust manufacturers failed to follow the Independents' example in seeking new Wall Street finance.

Above all the inflexibility of the organization constructed by the MPPC prevented it from adapting to the new conditions produced by the arrival of the multireel film. A final nail in the coffin came with the First World War and the loss of the European markets, which the Trust manufacturers had cultivated more assiduously than had the Independents.

Apart from its efforts to bring order and standardization into the film industry, the Motion Picture Patents Company took upon itself the moral purification of the movies. *The Moving Picture World* which, while asserting its independence, was curiously subservient to the Trust in its early days, wrote in July 1909:

> It can truly be said that if some such force as the Motion Picture Patents Company had not come into existence last year, conditions at the present time would have been so bad that the very existence of the moving picture itself would have been jeopardized. All over the coun-

try you had the public conscience revolting against the display of unsuitable, degrading, demoralizing, obscene pictures. You had the press antagonistic to the moving picture; you had the clergy similarly hostile; you had municipal authorities all over the United States avowedly unfavorable to the nickelodeon; you had overcrowded and bad theaters; in fact you had about as bad a condition of business as could be imagined.

These assertions appear more remarkable when compared with the views expressed in an editorial in the same magazine only seven months earlier, at the very moment when the Motion Picture Patents Company was coming into being:

The extensive support given by the public to the moving picture shows proves that, in the main, they are of a nature that is elevating, for the great American public are not fools. At the same time [the writer added mildly enough], the public morals should be considered, the public health by proper ventilation, and the public safety by simple means of exit in case of panic.

This editorial was in fact a reaction to a startling development that had just taken place. On Christmas Eve 1908 the mayor of New York, George B. McClellan, abruptly revoked the license of every moving picture show in the city. His stated reason was a concern for safety:

"I feel personally responsible for the safety and lives of the patrons and take this action on personal knowledge of existing conditions and the firm conviction that I am averting a public calamity." The exhibitors however suspected that the mayor had yielded to representations from clergy protesting about the immorality of cinema shows: one for instance had recently condemned the protagonist's tunic in Vitagraph's Julius Caesar for revealing too much of his knees.

The Moving Picture World suspected deeper involvements:

There are excellent reasons for the belief that the crisis the picture men have been forced to meet was not brought about entirely by the clergy. That they have been used as a catspaw by one of the strong organizations of vaudeville exhibitors is accepted as a fact in many quarters. For several weeks it has been known that the organization of actors has been formulating plans to put the moving pictures out of business. If they did not succeed in getting the clergy to do the trick, their labors,

THE AGENT

■ A cartoon in *Moving Picture World* portrayed the industry's reaction to the chilling effect of local crusades to close theaters and restrict the showing of movies on moral grounds (left). Led by the Trust, producers and exhibitors emphasized wholesome family fare as an antidote to criticism and censorship. The Cascade Theater, established in 1906, in the factory town of New Castle, Pennsylvania, by the brothers Harry and Sam Warner, offered "refined entertainment for Ladies, Gentlemen—and—Children" (right).

and the results accomplished through the Mayor's order at least form a striking coincident.

Like any entertainment appropriated by the masses, the nickelodeon was bound to attract the attention of puritans and reformers. Eileen Bowser quotes the striking phrase of a feminist reformer, "These places are the recruiting stations of vice." The darkened halls and throng of children and young girls set off the alarms of prurience.

The criticisms were however always more than offset by the views of social workers like Jane Addams of Chicago and many clergy who used films for the entertainment and education of their congregations. Advocates of popular education welcomed one-reel efforts that introduced the works of Shakespeare, Dickens, Scott, Tolstoy, and Browning to the masses.

If it is hard to discover the widespread enmity *The Moving Picture World* alleged, in defense of the efforts of the MPPC, it is even harder to find much evidence of the "unsuitable, degrading, demoralizing, obscene pictures." It is true that by American standards of the day, some of the French imports seemed a trifle saucy or violent. From time to time a sensational film like Lubin's *The Unwritten Law*, which dramatized the Thaw–White murder case while it was still before the courts, attracted odium as well as sell-out theaters. Yet *The Moving Picture World*'s editorial brought a *cri de coeur* from an exhibitor in Richmond, Virginia., who begged to be put in touch with some exchange that could furnish some of the objectionable films of which there was so much talk, since his patrons "want these sort of subjects." He added hopefully that he might be able to buy up some of them very cheap now that the demand had lessened. In the whole career of *The Moving Picture World* only a single advertisement hinted at the availability of out-and-out erotica, and the promise of a "Pikante Herrenabend Program" was discreetly obscured by German language.

Mayor McClellan's closure of the New York theaters did not last long. The exhibitors, led by William Fox, quickly obtained an injunction that permitted them to reopen. The incident struck alarm, however, bringing the message that unless the industry made a show of putting its house in order, others would undertake the task. "At the hearing before the Mayor last week," said *The Moving Picture World*, "the manufacturers offered to pay for the services of a censor. . . If a censorship of all films is decided upon, the manufacturer, the renter and the exhibitor should be represented as well as the public."

The progressive People's Institute in New York announced plans for a censorship board in March 1909. The Motion Picture Patents Company enthusiastically supported the move as a means of self-censorship, and the National Board of Censorship was established. The Board quite quickly lost its influence, however, as an increasing number of states introduced their own censorship, overriding the generally liberal and intelligent judgments of the National Board.

The Motion Picture Patents Company undertook the task of reform with a will. Eileen Bowser comments ironically that "To uplift, ennoble and purify was good business too. Progressive idealism did not conflict with their ideas of how to expand the market." To appear as redeemers of this fallen industry was a sure way to appeal to every sector of the industry and of society at large. *The Moving Picture World*'s sensational picture of the horrors of 1907 from which, in the nick of time, the Trust had rescued industry and public alike reads suspiciously like part of the Trust's own publicity campaign.

The Trust years saw a very conscious and unembarrassed uplift effort throughout much of the industry. The trade magazines carried endless articles on educational films. Other companies followed the Edison policy of collaborating with social institutions in the production of message melodramas. For a year or two the melodrama of moral sentiment and instructive dénouement took over from low comedy with its irresponsible fun. A large part of the repertory of the day had a dispiriting seriousness of purpose.

For a radical historian like Lewis Jacobs, writing in the Roosevelt years, the Trust represented the ugliest and most repressive aspects of capitalism and industrial monopoly. Later historians, with a benevolent nostalgia for nineteenth-century entrepreneurist capitalism, have endeavored to revise that view. Robert Anderson, from the perspective of 1985, believed that:

> From 1909 until its court-ordered demise in 1915, the MPPC radically altered, upgraded, and codified American film production, distribution, and exhibition. The Patents Company was responsible for ending the foreign domination of American screens, increasing film quality through internal competition, and standardizing film distribution and exhibition practices. But, and perhaps more significant, by aligning the small disorganized film companies into a combination of licensed manufacturers, the MPPC succeeded in transforming the fledgling American motion picture business into an international competitive industry.

Most of these assertions are individually questionable. A no less defensible view might be that the chaos and confusion of the industry before the formation of the Trust resulted largely from the constant threat of Edison litigation. The Trust period proper brought an era of bitter conflict on the one hand, and stultifying standardization on the other, effectively hindering the processes of evolution which would have been natural to an art in the process of discovery and an industry under the stimuli of booming business and competition.

8

PRODUCTION AND THE WAY WEST

The migration to California

THROUGHOUT THE EARLY YEARS, AMERICAN FILM PRO-
duction was based in the East. The pioneer companies had built their studios
in New York, all in time conforming to the same natural drift from the center
of the city to the fringes. Thus in 1901 Edison moved production from Orange
to East 21st Street; and then in 1907 opened a studio in the Bronx. American
Mutoscope and Biograph opened premises at 841 Broadway (the opposite side
of Union Square from Edison), but then in 1903 moved a block away to 14th
Street, eventually following Edison to the Bronx in 1913. Vitagraph began in
Manhattan, on Nassau Street, but moved to Brooklyn in 1906. Later came the
New York Motion Picture Company and Laemmle's IMP. By 1912, New Jersey was the home of Nestor, Champion, Pathé, Solax, Eclair, and Victor. Selig
and Essanay were in Chicago, Sigmund Lubin in Philadelphia.

Early historians attributed the westward migration that began toward the
end of the first decade of the century to the influence of the Trust. Terry
Ramsaye wrote, "The pressure of the Patents Company's attack on the
Independents was a contributing factor to the development of motion picture
geography in this period. Independent picture making activities in and about
New York were beset by difficulties. Cameras vanished from under the noses
of the guards. Mysterious chemical accidents happened in the laboratories,
resulting in the loss of costly negatives. The fight was not confined to the
courts."

Since Ramsaye was writing quite close to the time, and personally knew
many of those involved, there is probably substance in this; but the Trust can
only have been, as he says, a contributing factor, for the Trust companies

■ The Biograph Studio, 14th Street, New York City. From 1903 until 1913, the American Mutoscope and Biograph Company (later just Biograph Company) made movies in this converted brownstone building located near Union Square and the resources of New York's theater district. Stages with artificial lighting were used for interior scenes. Exteriors were filmed in a variety of nearby neighborhoods and the countryside around the city.

were as much involved in the migration as the Independents. Certainly another persuasive reason was the short winter days of the Eastern cities. Most of the manufacturers (as film production companies were then invariably styled) had well-equipped glass-house studios; yet even with auxiliary artificial lighting, the sunless winter days severely restricted filming.

California was not the first or the only region where filmmakers looked for better light. For a while it seemed that Jacksonville, Florida, might become the filmmaking center of the states; and indeed the city advertised itself as "The World's Winter Film Capital." Kalem, Majestic, Thanhouser, Selig, Lubin, and the Gene Gauntier Feature Players all set up winter production there. In 1910 both Edison and IMP wintered in Cuba.

The most inveterate traveler among the Patents Companies however was Kalem, perhaps because it had no permanent studio of its own. The company went regularly to Jacksonville, where it specialized in Civil War stories. In 1910 and 1911 the Kalem crew twice ventured to Europe and earned the nickname of the O'Kalems with its Irish subjects, which included *A Lad From Old Ireland* and *The Colleen Bawn*. In the winter of 1911–12 the company was in the Holy Land where it made its greatest success, *From the Manger to the Cross*.

The lure of California could not long be resisted though. A newsman of the time extolled its attractions: "Clear air and sunshine are available three hundred days out of the year, perfect conditions for picture making. The scenic advantages are unique. From the heights of Edendale one can see the Pacific Ocean and the broad panorama of Southern California with its fruit and stock ranches, its snow-capped mountains and its tropical vegetation to the east, north and south. Within a short distance of Edendale may be found every known variety of national scenery, seemingly arranged by a master producer expressly for the motion picture camera. In this enchanted land are produced those startling and spectacular westerns that so enchant the movie audiences."

It was a Trust company that first began serious production in California. In 1908 Francis Boggs, a talented director taken on by the Selig Polyscope Company the previous year, traveled to California to film exteriors for *Monte Cristo*. Some scenes were shot at Laguna and Venice beaches, but other sets were built on a rooftop, over a building in downtown Los Angeles. With all the space and sunlight that filmmakers could wish for, the old habits of urban filmmaking still died hard. Boggs shot another film, *The Cattle Rustlers*, in the West, and the following year rented a lot behind the Sing Loo Chinese laundry, where he shot *The Heart of a Race Track Tout*, with location scenes at the Santa Anita track. By this time Colonel Selig had authorized the

■ Jacksonville vied with Los Angeles as a production location during months when northern cities were cold and dark. The always mobile Kalem Company was photographed in Jacksonville, Florida, about 1910. Left to right: Max Schneider (cameraman), Kenean Buel (actor and, later, director), James Vincent (leading man), Quincy "the high diver" (the black child), Gene Gauntier (actress and scriptwriter), Mrs. Schneider, Ben Owen, Tom Santley, Minerva Florence, and Sidney Olcott (director).

building of a permanent studio at 1845 Allessandro Avenue in Edendale. In 1911 Selig further extended his Hollywood holdings by building a new studio and zoo at 3900 Mission Road.

The first of the Independents, the New York Motion Picture Company, arrived out West in November 1909. The original company was managed by Fred Balshofer and headed by James Young Deer and Princess Red Wing. In 1912 the company, under the gifted direction of Thomas Ince and with a new name, Bison, took over an area in the Santa Ynez canyon and hired a company of the Miller Brothers 101 Ranch Wild West Show. Mack Sennett was put in charge of the company's original Edendale studio, which became Keystone.

G. M. Anderson—"Bronco Billy" as well as the "A" of Essanay—set out westward to find more realistic settings for westerns than Chicago could offer. He tried Colorado, Texas, and Mexico before settling on Niles, California, where Essanay set up its Western studio in 1910.

Early that year Biograph's star director, D. W. Griffith, brought a company to Los Angeles, and instantly responded to the opportunity presented by the landscapes. The films he made on this trip included *Ramona* and *The Unchanging Sea*. He was back the following January with a larger unit and set up studio and laboratory facilities. The California sojourns grew still longer and more productive in 1912 and 1913, when Griffith finally quit Biograph to work independently in California.

The first purpose-built studio in Hollywood was established in the winter of 1911 by the Nestor Company, on Gower and Sunset. The Universal Company occupied a site opposite on Gower Street, although the following

■   Attracted by favorable weather and a variety of locations, Selig Company sent director Francis Boggs to California, where he filmed exteriors for *Monte Cristo* in 1908 (above left). Selig returned to Los Angeles regularly and eventually established a studio in Edendale. In 1910, Hollywood was a small community on the fringe of Los Angeles (above right). Groves of orange and lemon trees were the principal landmarks. The building with the small dome at the center of the photograph was a residence and is now the home of the American Society of Cinematographers. David Horsley built the first studio in Hollywood in the winter of 1911. This is a panoramic view of Nestor's players and crew members who came to Hollywood from Bayonne, N.J. (above).

year Carl Laemmle chose a deserted valley location on Lankershim Boulevard to create the permanent Universal Studios, officially opened in 1915. In 1913 Jesse Lasky and Samuel Goldfish (later Goldwyn) leased a farm at Selma and Vine, which became a studio for Cecil B. De Mille to shoot *The Squaw Man*. By 1913 every major company except for Edison was working either permanently or during the winters in California.

■ Cowboys and Indians of the Bison Company on location in New Jersey in 1909 (above left), James Young Deer and his wife, Princess Red Wing (on right), and Evelyn Graham (center). The couple on the left are unidentified. The Bison Company migrated to California later in 1909, because audiences no longer believed that New Jersey looked like the West. G. M. Anderson, partner with George Spoor in the Essanay Company (S. and A. for Spoor and Anderson) was the first popular cowboy star. Anderson moved from Chicago to Niles, California, to film his Broncho Billy westerns. This is a scene from *Broncho Billy Anderson in Broncho Billy's Adventure* (Essanay 1911) (above right). An unlikely hero, Anderson lacked traditional cowboy skills and had to be taught to ride, but his fans liked him and he played the amiable Broncho Billy for several years.

The effect of California upon American cinema was profound. The variety of spectacular scenery and the vastness of the horizon liberated filmmakers from the narrow visions of rooftop studio settings. A whole new range of subjects became possible—historical, western, rural, marine—and the settings permitted a new level of realism. Filmgoers could never again be satisfied with the narrow and scrubby simulated Wild West of New Jersey.

Directors and cameramen responded with excitement to the pictorial possibilities of mountain tops, endless plains, limitless skies, the sunlit sea. Filming the spectacle of horses and riders sweeping over the prairies liberated the camera to discover a new flamboyance and dynamism. The new films from the West introduced filmgoers all over the world to places and visions such as they had never seen before, and with which no other country could compete. In California Americans discovered a native art form.

9

TELLING STORIES

Development of film narrative

THE SECOND DECADE OF MOTION PICTURES, FROM 1903 to 1913, witnessed the creation of a new narrative medium. In 1903 even the most advanced story films, like Porter's *The Great Train Robbery*, still retained much of the method of animated lantern slides. Ten years later films such as *Judith of Bethulia* or *Traffic in Souls* deployed a new, supple, and quite autonomous art.

The nickelodeon explosion provided a significant impetus. The demand for new films was insatiable; and audiences made it plain that what they wanted was stories. The interest films and travel films and one-point gags persisted, but as time went on the well-balanced show was expected to provide a melodrama, a comedy, and a western. From the magic lantern era, early film exhibitors had inherited the lecturer, who would link and explain the films. In time the lecturer was replaced by explanatory titles either projected by a separate lantern or included in the film itself: the Edison Company, advertising Porter's *Uncle Tom's Cabin* (1903), announced "In this film we have made a departure from the old method of dissolving one scene into another by inserting announcements with brief descriptions as they appear in succession." Descriptive titles can have had little attraction for the run of nickelodeon patrons though, while the commercial hurly-burly involved in a daily change of program and a show every half hour did not provide a comfortable task for lecturers.

Showmen and public alike began to recognize that the best films were those which told their stories so clearly through the pictures that no extraneous explanation was required. One obvious way to achieve this was to tell stories that everyone already knew; but with the daily program change the supply of familiar tales like *Uncle Tom's Cabin*, *Ten Nights in a Bar Room*, or *The Pied Piper of Hamelin* was soon to run out. Filmmakers had to find original stories—or at least to disguise the old ones—and learn to tell them lucidly and expressively.

This was easiest if the story was simple to tell and simple to follow; and these conditions were ideally fulfilled by the chase film, which flourished internationally as a genre in its own right in the years 1903–1906. All that was required was to establish some offense—a theft, an insult, or a boy's naughtiness—and then launch a pursuit after the offender. The pursuit could be extended ad infinitum, through any number of successive scenes and situations.

As filmmakers devised variations, and stole ideas from one another, the chase proved a valuable exercise in film style. The movement provided its own visual dynamism, and conventions developed which advanced concepts of shot relation. It was usual for instance to have the chased and chasers exit the shot by running forward, past the camera, sometimes producing stimulating variations of composition. The incidents that motivated the chases were in time elaborated, to become stories in themselves.

Thus Biograph made *Personal* (1904), the story of an aristocratic Frenchman who advertises that he will meet any prospective wives at Grant's Tomb, and finds himself fleeing from a horde of eager spinsters. The film was such a hit that it was quickly plagiarized, often with interesting elaborations, by Edison (snappily titled *How a French Nobleman Got a Wife Through the New York Herald Personal Columns*), by Lubin and in France by Pathé. Years later Buster Keaton, who had no doubt seen one or another of the variants as a child touring in vaudeville, revived the plot for *Seven Chances*.

Film style was generally dominated by the standard set-up inherited as much from the conventions of composition of magic lantern slides as from the theater. The action was played behind a line twelve feet from the camera lens, which was generally placed at about chest height. This formal staging, with the actors shown at full length, was sometimes varied however by novelty effects. Very early in the century the English director G. A. Smith cut into his films shots showing the view that the film's main character saw through a magnifying glass (*Grandma's Reading Glass*) or a telescope (*As Seen Through a Telescope*), or a closer view of a character (*Mary Jane's Mishap*). Edwin S. Porter developed the insert idea in a smoother and more filmic way in *The Gay Shoe Clerk* (1903) when he cut to a close-up detail of the young man of the title toying with the ankle of a woman customer.

About 1903, a temporary truce in the legal wrangling over copyrights and patents gave the big companies more time and resources to devote to film-

■ The American Mutoscope and Biograph Company popularized the chase film with *Personal* (1904), a comedy about a Frenchman overwhelmed by a motley mob of women after he advertises for a wife (above left). Edison and Lubin made essentially identical versions. Edison's *How a French Nobleman Got a Wife Through the New York Herald Personal Columns* also opens at Grant's Tomb in New York (below left). Lubin's *Meet Me at the Fountain* opens in front of a fountain in Philadelphia (below right). In each film the comedy is provided by a cross-country chase with the women in pursuit of the fleeing Frenchman. The similar films offer an unusual opportunity to compare the work of Billy Bitzer, who shot *Personal*, and Edwin S. Porter, director-cameraman of *How a French Nobleman.*

making. Edison resumed full-scale production while Biograph opened a new indoor studio at 11 East 14th Street, where artificial lighting was used for the first time. More and more multishot films were being made. Biograph put together a series of separate films of Joseph Jefferson as Rip Van Winkle, which had been shot seven years before, to make a continuous narrative. In *The American Soldier in Love and War* it assembled war actualities and staged

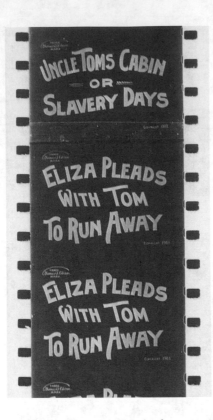

■ Longer films stimulated innovation to make them more comprehensible and pleasing. Edwin S. Porter's *Uncle Tom's Cabin* (Edison 1903) is one of the earliest films using title frames with text to help the audience understand its story (above left). In *A Search for Evidence* (American Mutoscope & Biograph 1903) Billy Bitzer used a keyhole-shaped mask on the camera's lens to make the viewer a participant in a voyeuristic search for a philandering husband (above right). Porter's *The Kleptomaniac* (Edison 1905) expressed outrage that a poor woman is jailed for stealing bread to feed her sick child while a wealthy shoplifter goes free (right).

scenes to make a unified story. Visual novelties included Biograph's *A Search for Evidence* (1903), an erotic variation on the chase idea, in which a wife and a detective in pursuit of an errant husband spy through keyholes upon the goings-on in a succession of hotel rooms: what they see is shown on screen within a keyhole-shaped mask. (The device had however been used in 1901 in Pathé's *Through the Keyhole*).

Edison's *The Great Train Robbery* and *Uncle Tom's Cabin* had firmly established the taste for longer narratives, based on theatrical favorites. Both films were instantly pirated by Sigmund Lubin, and other filmmakers entered the story film field. Selig produced *The Pied Piper of Hamelin* and *Scenes from Humpty Dumpty* (1903), which was advertised as being "posed for by one of the greatest European Pantomimists"; presumably the film was inspired by the spectacular Drury Lane Humpty Dumpty of the same year.

Under the direction of the lively Wallace McCutcheon, Biograph embarked on regular production of story films, and introduced intertitles as a permanent feature. Some of the clever little films it made in 1904 were the prototypes of plots that would continue to be elaborated in many later films. *The Suburbanite*, a comedy about the catastrophes of a family induced to attempt to settle in the suburbs, parodied the publicity of a railroad company's advertising magazine of the same name. *The Moonshiner* presented an antiromantic view of the deprivations of rural life.

In 1905 the Edison Company enticed into its service McCutcheon and several other Biograph staff after which Edison's story-film program became distinctly livelier as Biograph's declined. Porter moved easily between comedy (*The Burglar's Slide for Life*, *Everybody Works But Father*, *The Whole Dam Family and the Dam Dog*) and melodramas like *The Ex-Convict* and *The Miller's Daughter*, and evinced a taste for stop-action animation (*The Teddy Bears*). Porter had a feeling for the strong sentiments of an uneducated and unsophisticated public, and appealed to an outraged sense of justice with *The Kleptomaniac*, which showed the different treatment that society metes out to a poor woman who steals a loaf of bread to feed her sick child, and to a rich shoplifter. Vitagraph became an important producer of story films. The background of one of its founders, J. Stuart Blackton, as a newspaper cartoonist, no doubt in part explains Vitagraph's sense of visual storytelling. Vitagraph tended to favor sophisticated established stage successes, like *Raffles the Amateur Cracksman* and *Monsieur Beaucaire*.

Other companies were coming to the fore. Alongside his canny plagiarism of the latest successes of others, Siegmund Lubin turned out highly efficient, technically brisk, spicy films admirably calculated to the audiences of the lower-class vaudeville houses. Selig titles like *Tracked by Bloodhounds or, A Lynching at Cripple Creek*, or *The Holdup of the Leadville Stage* promised lurid thrills.

The medium was however to be transformed, in the course of five years, by one man, David Wark Griffith. Historians have gnawed upon Griffith's great reputation, criticized his limited aesthetic horizons and his

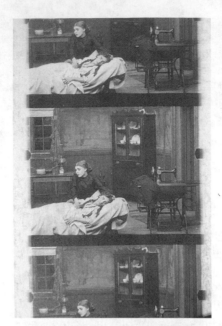
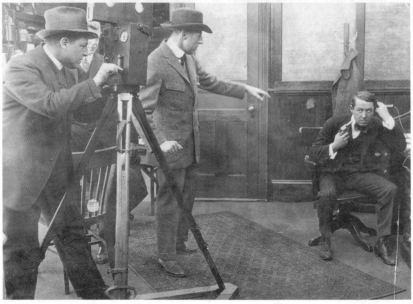

■ D. W. Griffith was America's most prominent pioneer film director. Here he is directing Henry B. Walthall in *Death's Marathon* (Biograph 1913) with Billy Bitzer at the camera (facing page below). The first movie directed by D. W. Griffith was Biograph's *The Adventures of Dollie*, filmed at Sound Beach, Connecticut, June 18 and 19, 1908 (facing page above right). It is the story of the coincidental rescue of a young girl who had been kidnapped by a vengeful gypsy. Arthur Johnson played the father, Linda Arvidson (Mrs. D. W. Griffith) the mother, and Charles Inslee the gypsy; Arthur Marvin was cameraman. In *Lonely Villa* (Biograph 1909) Griffith built tension by cutting between scenes of the attacking burglars, the trapped women, and the husband desperately rushing to the rescue (above). Mary Pickford and Adele De Garde are the children, and Marion Leonard is the frantic mother telephoning her husband. In *The Song of the Shirt* (Biograph 1908), one of several Griffith films with strong social themes, Florence Lawrence plays a poverty-stricken young woman sewing shirts at home in a futile effort to save her dying sister (Linda Arvidson) (facing page above left). Their struggle is starkly contrasted with the affluent hedonism of an exploiting clothing manufacturer.

---

political capriciousness, quite accurately traced antecedents for every device that was credited to his invention. His achievement still remains unassailable. He discovered the whole potential of an art. He was a storyteller on the scale of the great Victorian novelists he admired. "He put beauty and poetry," said his disciple Erich von Stroheim, "into a cheap and tawdry sort of amusement."

Griffith was born in 1875 into a Southern family that had been ruined by the Civil War. His early career alternated between modest acting jobs and humiliating fill-in work. His persistent literary ambitions seemed to be fulfilled when his play *A Fool and a Girl* was staged with the great actress Fanny Ward; but when it was a flop, the impoverished Griffith slunk off to find work in the movies—still the ultimate shame for a self-respecting legitimate actor.

At Edison, Porter rejected a scenario in which Griffith plagiarized *Tosca*, but gave him a part in a melodrama, *Rescued from an Eagle's Nest*. Four days' work on this having perhaps improved his skills (his wife claimed he had never actually seen a film at the time) Griffith had better luck selling scenarios to Biograph. In the summer of 1908 he directed his first film, *The Adventures of Dollie*.

In the course of the next five years Griffith directed or supervised more than four hundred films at Biograph. Inevitably many were repetitive and stereotyped, yet overall they were superior in technique and content to anything that had gone before. Audiences all over the world recognized something new and thrilling in these films, and the failing fortunes of Biograph were triumphantly revived.

Griffith certainly did not consciously set out to make a revolution. He aimed only to tell stories; but he was a great storyteller, able to fuse what he had absorbed from the Victorian art he loved—the great novels, the romantic poetry and painting of the pre-Raphaelite taste—and gifted with a passionate instinct for manipulating moving images which enabled him to seize upon and discover all the untried possibilities the cinema offered.

The great discovery at which he would arrive, bit by bit, was that a scene could be split up into small fragments, incomplete in themselves, out of which the whole could be reassembled. This, he recognized, gave him much more command of dramatic and emotional effect. He could provide emphasis through the composition and framing of his images, by the placing and movement of the camera, and most important by the juxtaposition of the images and the speed and rhythm with which they were edited.

Griffith broke the "twelve-foot" convention, which used the screen like a proscenium arch. Working from his love of Victorian painting, he used composition, and showed that the screen image was not just two-dimensional but had a background and foreground. By 1910 he was varying the shot, freely using close-up or extreme long shot within the same scene. In collaboration with Bitzer he devised ways of masking the screen, or using irises, for particular emphasis. He encouraged Bitzer to experiment with realistic or impressionistic effects of light and shade.

■ At the Biograph Company, D. W. Griffith inherited a talented stable of performers which he enhanced by recruiting and training some of the industry's best-known talents. Biograph players Henry B. Walthall (below left) and Mae Marsh (above left) starred in *The Birth of a Nation* and other later productions by Griffith. Blanche Sweet (above right) was one of the industry's most popular leading ladies.

After only four months at Biograph, Griffith made the revolutionary leap of cutting within a scene, in his first adaptation of *Enoch Arden*, *After Many Years*. Moreover the cut from a shot of the heroine to her shipwrecked husband was linked not by dramatic logic, but by the subjective thought connection of a character. Griffith justified it to his doubtful employers by pointing out that this was the way that Dickens wrote—an anticipation of Sergei Eisenstein's study of parallels between prose writing and montage.

In *Lonely Villa*, Griffith first used a technique he was to make famous, cutting between two separate and parallel actions in order to build up suspense and drama. As he developed the method, using the pace of his cutting to pitch up the excitement, he showed how the editing process could manipulate time and space in a way which was impossible in the live theater.

Griffith's increasing use of close-up enabled him to use actors in a far more expressive way than was possible with the old long-shot proscenium technique. He assembled and trained a company of very young actors and actresses—Mary Pickford, Lillian and Dorothy Gish, Mae Marsh, Blanche Sweet, Henry B. Walthall, Marion Leonard, Florence Lawrence, and Robert Harron—whose faces were unblemished and whose technique was not yet marked by habit. He taught them to avoid the excessive gesture of early screen pantomime and to interiorize their performances.

As well as its technique, Griffith enlarged the repertoire of the cinema. Inevitably, with his huge output of one-reel films at Biograph, his work was eclectic, including melodramas, westerns, thrillers, sentimental romances, historical themes, and even comedy (which was always Griffith's Achilles heel, in life as in art). Yet within his first months at Biograph he was giving the American public Browning and Tennyson as well as the safer literary favorites like Dickens, Poe, and Shakespeare. In *The Song of the Shirt* (1908) and *A Corner in Wheat* (1909), which was based on two stories by Frank Norris, he took on tough social themes, as he was to do even more effectively in his formidable crime story *The Musketeers of Pig Alley* (1912). Naive as their pretensions may seem eighty years later, films like *Judith of Bethulia* and *Man's Genesis* gave the cinema new intellectual status. When Griffith left Biograph in 1913, already planning *The Birth of a Nation*, which was to prove the most influential (and, with its unarguably racist content, the most controversial) film in cinema history, he was the undisputed master of the screen. He had transformed the art, and no filmmaker in the entire world was to be unaffected by his discoveries and achievement.

INTERNATIONAL RIVALRIES

The United States and Europe struggle for market domination

NO OTHER CULTURAL FORM AND NO ONE NATION HAS ever, in the whole course of history, achieved such dominance as the American cinema enjoys in the world today. American styles, values, virtues, and vices are promoted wherever films are shown, and exert profound influence, for good or ill, upon impressionable audiences throughout the world. The foundations of this hegemony were laid in the first twenty years of motion pictures, which saw a constantly shifting but eventually decisive struggle for supremacy between the cinemas of the United States and Europe.

The universal appeal of motion pictures was recognized from the very beginning. The phonograph had already shown Edison the possibilities of international exploitation, and within months of its first appearance the Kinetoscope was being commercially exploited in Europe. No doubt exploitation of the Kinetoscope was accelerated by the urgency to beat imitators to the profits, since the invention was unprotected by foreign patents. No doubt, too, Dickson's cosmopolitan birthright gave him a heightened perception of the European market. Subsequently Dickson himself returned to Britain to head the London branch of Biograph—the first American film production company to open a permanent foreign branch.

Soon however the traffic was reversed. We have seen that the film that made the greatest impression at the first Vitascope show was an import from Britain—Robert W. Paul's *Rough Sea at Dover*. The first European cameras, by Lumière and Paul, were much lighter and more portable than those of Edison and Biograph; and for a while European actuality films could offer more exotic and varied scenes and sights.

At the opening of the century the most important filmmaker in the world, in terms of artistic enterprise, was the Frenchman Georges Méliès. Méliès' magic films and story films enjoyed tremendous success in the vaudeville theaters of the United States, but American film manufacturers assuaged any feelings of hurt chauvinism by copying and pirating them with shameless enthusiasm.

In order to defend himself, in the summer of 1903 Méliès opened an office of his Star Film Company at 204 East 38th Street, New York. He declared war on the unscrupulous American manufacturers who "found it easier and more economical fraudulently to copy the Star films and to advertise these poor copies as their own original conceptions. . . . In opening a factory and office in New York we are prepared and determined energetically to pursue all counterfeiters and pirates. We will not speak twice, we will act."

At about the same time the Pathé Company opened a New York office; and with films like *Sleeping Beauty* (1903), *Don Quixote* (1903), and *Christopher Columbus* (1904) began seriously to rival Méliès' successes. Fewer films were imported from Britain, though such imports of 1903 as Paul's *Trailed by Bloodhounds*, Walter Haggar's *A Desperate Poaching Affray*, and the Sheffield Photo Company's *A Daring Daylight Burglary* not only thrilled their audiences, but offered American filmmakers notable examples of fluid editing techniques.

The nickelodeon boom found American film manufacturers, disorganized by the constant menace of Edison patent litigation, quite unable to meet the dramatically increased demand. By 1907 it was estimated that two-thirds of the films released in the United States came from Europe, mainly France, Italy, and Scandinavia. Pathé of France, by that time the greatest film company in the world, was said to be supplying to America an average of more than one film per day, and as many as 75 prints of each title.

While Pathé had its own organization in the United States, other European firms such as Gaumont, Eclipse, Theo Pathé, and the London-based Charles Urban were importing their productions through agents like George Kleine. The flourishing import business encouraged other agencies, like that of the Miles Brothers, to open offices in London and Paris.

Although the French films were generally acknowledged to be superior in style and production values, many serious Americans were alarmed at such exposure to European morals. There were complaints against undress, the vulgarity of slapstick comedies and the general moral tone. "More often than not," fulminated *The Moving Picture World* in November 1909, "European films handle the sixth commandment too freely and therefore the subject is unsuitable for the average American audience. For this has to be said for

American manufacturers, that even in the darkest days of the brutal and criminal film, they stopped short of the gilded obscenity and veiled indecency of many imported films."

The reputation of French films however was substantially retrieved by the rise and importation of the "film d'art." This was a name and a strategy adopted by Pathé to attract a better-off and better-educated audience to the cinema. Scripts were commissioned from well-known writers or adapted from classic sources, and the best stage actors were recruited to perform them. In America Pathé earned prestige with films like *The Assassination of the Duke of Guise* (1908) and *The Great Breach* (1909), after Balzac's *La Grande Bretèche*. The genre became prestigious enough to be guyed. Nestor advertised "Films d'Luxe" and Laemmle, "Films d'IMP."

An editorial in *The Moving Picture World* warned manufacturers that exchanges were importing films because the public was rejecting the inadequate quality of many home-produced independent films. In particular the East Coast westerns were targeted: "Your exchange man who can only get pictures of Western subjects against Eastern backgrounds is wise to the game. So he goes elsewhere—that is abroad —and gets the real thing."

Realism, even when subjects were fantastic or mythical, was now the quality most demanded of films. The audiences wanted above all to be convinced by the reality of what they saw on the screen. This was ideally achieved by the costly and grandiose spectacle films that began to arrive from Italy. A leader on "The Qualities of Imported Film" in *The Moving Picture World* (November 6, 1909) extolled the Italian producer Arturo Ambrosio's *Nerone*, released as *Nero and the Burning of Rome*:

> We sat in simple amazement at the marvelous manner in which the production had been staged, artistically dressed, lighted and photographed. We seemed, for all the world, to be looking on a production of Mansfield, Irving or some great producing actor who is determined to give the public a chef d'oeuvre. It was no simple comedy scene, but one demanding all the magnificent effects of ancient Rome shown with perfect literality. Gorgeousness of procession, brilliancy of costume and acting, and finally the great conflagration of Rome; such a marvelous realism of effect that as we sat and watched this colored part of the film we seemed, as it were, to hear the cries of the victims.

The scale of such productions amazed American producers, but when an interviewer for *The Moving Picture World* mentioned their cost to Ambrosio he was vehement: "Money! There you are! American—money. Money—

American. We do not take cost into consideration in making our pictures. We set out to attain a desired result—and we get it." This was a clear rebuke to the factory methods of the Trust.

The vogue for Italian spectacles grew and boomed. In April 1911 the Sales Company released Itala Films' *The Fall of Troy*, directed by Giovanni Pastrone. The liberated camera style as well as the spectacle and lavish production was a revelation for American filmmakers and audiences. This was followed in November by Cines' *The Crusaders, or Jerusalem Delivered*, in 4 reels. By 1912 Ambrosio had established his own office in New York to distribute *Satan, or The Drama of Humanity* and *The Life of Dante*.

Pliny P. Craft, a former publicity man for Buffalo Bill's Wild West Show, imported two epic productions by the Milano Company—*Dante's Inferno* and *Homer's Odyssey*. The films were exhibited in 1912 in roadshow presentations, in legitimate theaters, with special music and sound effects. For "the famous $200,000 dollar production" *Homer's Odyssey*, Craft anticipated later styles of marketing campaign, with an eight-page color supplement (the first of its kind) in *The Moving Picture World*, souvenir program, merchandising novelties and $2 tickets.

Italian spectacle films went on to new triumph in April 1913, when George Kleine launched the Cines production *Quo Vadis* as a roadshow presentation in major legitimate theaters throughout the United States. The premiere run was at the Astor Theater, New York, where a Wurlitzer organ, said the *New York Herald*, "discoursed sacred compositions at intervals and imitated the roaring of a lion." The advertising was unprecedented, with posters up to 32-sheet size.

The success of *Quo Vadis* led to a production contract between Kleine and Ambrosio, which resulted in *The Last Days of Pompeii*, *The Betrothed*, and *Othello*. After a further triumph with Cines' *Anthony and Cleopatra*, Kleine embarked on a scheme to build his own studio on the outskirts of Turin, but this pioneer enterprise for American production in Europe was frustrated by the outbreak of the European War.

While Italy sent America spectacle films, France sent Bernhardt. The Divine Sarah had remained a legend in the United States since her American debut in 1880 at the age of 36. Thirty years on, her appearance in the four-reel *Queen Elizabeth* could still be advertised as "the film sensation of the age"; and the picture—stodgy and unflattering to its star as it was—made a fortune for Adolph Zukor. Two other Bernhardt films, *Tosca* (made in 1908) and *Adrienne Lecouvreur* followed in rapid succession in the winter of 1912–13.

■ *Homer's Odyssey*, a "Film Classic of the Ages," imported by Pliny P. Craft in 1912, was among the first of a number of popular Italian-made feature-length historical spectacles.

The Eclectic Film Company, the unlicensed arm of Pathé, established to exploit state rights of feature films, advertised portentously in 1913 that "On Tuesday, April 1, the French Line Steamer `La Touraine' will arrive in America with the Greatest Motion Picture Production Ever Made, *Les Misérables*." Later Eclectic releases included *Nero* and *Britannicus*.

Not all the successful imports were spectacles and classics. In 1913 Union Features released Eclair's *Balaoo the Demon Baboon* and the sensational thriller serial *Zigomar*, while Gaumont, with their own offices in Flushing, New York, distributed Louis Feuillade's thriller masterpiece *Fantomas*.

Italy and France dominated the import market. One of the rare German films of this period to reach America, the Continental Kunstfilm Company's film, *The Miracle*. Karl Volmoller's "wordless miracle spectacle" gave the American public its first glimpse of a Max Reinhardt stage production.

By this time, however, the traffic was beginning to reverse, as American production increased and exports outweighed imports. In the year between June 1911 and June 1912 exports of positive film were reported to have been 80 million feet against 14 million feet imported. This figure is misleading, however, since European firms tended only to send negatives to America, and then make positive prints on arrival, in order to save on heavy tariffs. American manufacturers could export multiple positives without problems. The European market became so important to American producers that most

DANIEL FROHMAN

PRESENTS

MME. SARAH
BERNHARDT

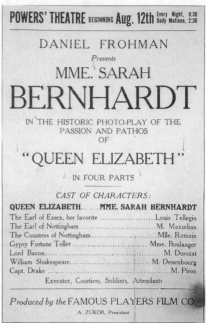

■ In 1912, theater-owner Adolph Zukor imported the French production of *Queen Elizabeth*, starring Sarah Bernhardt (above left and right). The film was stagey and the camera was unkind to the aging actress, but Zukor's career was launched. One of the earliest and most popular serials was Louis Feuillade's *Fantomas*, produced and imported by the Gaumont Company in 1912 (left).

of the major companies opened offices in London, which was the center for European distribution.

Significantly this turnaround coincided with the start of the industry's move to Hollywood. The dramatic scenery of California gave to American films spectacle and realism with which even the Italians could not compete. The breadth and grandeur of the locations and the novelty of their new subjects stimulated Californian filmmakers to new, freer, more exciting styles of using the medium. At the same time D. W. Griffith demonstrated new forms and new power of storytelling.

By 1913 American films had begun to exert a hold over the audiences of the world that would never be relinquished. In the summer of 1913 W. Stephen Bush of *The Moving Picture World* embarked on a tour of Europe. American films, he found, still failed to impress Italian audiences, while the French displayed their notorious chauvinism "as if the motto were: French films for French audiences. Today mighty few films are sold in France." Even so, "of the foreign films sold, the Americans are well in the lead."

For German audiences, however, Bush reported, "the screened description of American life, American customs and manners, American men, women, and children seem to be specially attractive. While we often discriminate against the foreign pictures, the foreigners seem to be prejudiced in favor of our pictures. American comedies are in great demand. . . . There is no reason why this market cannot yield as fine returns to the American producer as the British market."

For in England, "the American film of today holds an easy supremacy over the rest. . . . The only films which seem to appeal to the British public are the products of either purely American or partly American films." Passing through Cecil Court in central London, where the film companies had their headquarters, he found Sam Warner in charge of the newly opened office of the Warner Feature Film Company. Warner told him, "this is an ideal market for an enterprising American picture man."

FEATURES AND PALACES

Revolutions in exhibition

THE ARRIVAL OF THE MULTIREEL FILMS FROM EUROPE accelerated an inevitable revolution in the American film industry, and thereby contributed to some degree to the demise of the Motion Picture Patents Company.

The rigid system of distribution and exhibition dominating the American industry and jealously maintained by the Trust was based upon the economy of one-reel films and standardized prices. (The length of one reel of film was 1,000 feet, representing a maximum running time of around 15 minutes.) In November 1909 *The Moving Picture World* declared confidently that "there is hardly a subject, except, perhaps, the Wagner unaccompanied opera, which cannot be, or has not been, shown on the moving picture screen by means of a thousand feet of film." Four years later the magazine admitted that "the two and three reel subject is indeed a necessary product of the higher ideal"; in other words, certain subjects could not be contained in the one-reel format, even though producers had gallantly tried with Tolstoy, Shakespeare, and Dickens.

Of the Trust manufacturers, Vitagraph was the first to devote more than one reel to important subjects with any regularity. A two-part *Life of Napoleon* was followed by a two-reel *Life of George Washington*, a four-reel *Les Misérables*, and a five-reel *Life of Moses*, all made in 1909. Later there were three-reel versions of *Uncle Tom's Cabin* (1910) and *A Tale of Two Cities* (1911), and a two-reel *Pickwick Papers* (1913).

However, the system resisted challenge. These films were released to the theaters in separate reels, one a week, and shown to the public as if they were

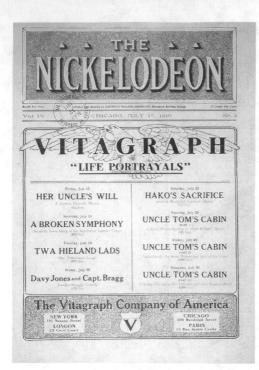

The Santa Maria, Nina and Pinta.

■ The Patents Company restricted production to one reel at a time, but its companies sometimes made longer films. Vitagraph's three-reel version of *Uncle Tom's Cabin* was released one reel at a time over a five-day period in July 1910 (above left). D. W. Griffith made a two-reel version of Tennyson's poem *Enoch Arden*, which was released by the Biograph Company one reel at a time, June 12 and 14, 1911 (below left). This is the description from *Biograph Bulletins,* which were published to advertise each film Biograph released. The descriptions often clarified complicated plots. *The Coming of Columbus* was the first multireel release by one of the Patents Companies (above right). Shot by Selig in Chicago, it used replicas of Columbus' ships built in 1893 for the Chicago World's Fair. Even after features became dominant, serials like *The Perils of Pauline* (Pathé 1914), starring the legendary Pearl White, suspended action at a moment of crisis in hopes of luring spectators to the next showing (facing page).

serials. When posters for individual films came into use around 1910, each individual reel was advertised by a separate poster. Only at special Sunday shows or in other favored situations might the licensed companies' multireel films occasionally be shown complete. At the Shubert Theater, New Orleans, for example, *The Life of Moses* was shown for eight days, with suitable sacred music.

The public and the press might protest, and the exchange men complain, but the system was, for the moment, immutable. Paradoxically, this curious method of releasing and showing multireel films a reel at a time was not wholly without positive side-effects. Faced with this peculiar constraint, the best filmmakers recognized the need to give each reel an individual dramatic integrity, a climax and the necessary suspense to provoke anticipation of the next episode: this was to have a lasting and beneficent influence on dramatic structure in American cinema. The reel-by-reel release may also have influenced the development of the American serial film. The rise of the serial is just outside the period under present review. The prototype, Selig's *The Adventures of Kathlyn*, made its appearance at the end of December 1913, to be followed in early 1914 by Edison's *Dollie of the Dailies* and Pathé's legendary *The Perils of Pauline*. The fashion for alliterative titles was thus established and duly observed by Pathé's subsequent *Exploits of Elaine* and Kalem's *Hazards of Helen*, the longest-running of all serials.

Since the distribution machinery of the Motion Picture Patents Trust was too inflexible to change in response to the new films arriving from Europe, it was generally left to the independents to import them and develop appropriate new styles of exhibition and marketing. In time multireel films came to be distinguished as "features," although in one-reeler days the term had been generally applied to any film that stood out from the rest in terms of special content, attractive title, or other qualities that could be "featured" in billing the show—the usage came from the "featured" attractions of vaudeville.

There were precedents—the Passion plays and prizefight films for example—for longer films requiring special marketing. In 1910 the box office furor over the multireel Johnson–Jeffries fight film inspired Pliny P. Craft to undertake a three-reel film of Buffalo Bill's Wild West Show, for which he had been a publicist. When the exchanges refused to handle the eventual film, *Buffalo Bill's Wild West and Pawnee Bill's Far East Show*, Craft used the same roadshow methods as the Wild West Show itself— booking legitimate theaters in large towns on a percentage agreement, and organizing his own presentation and publicity.

Craft's example was followed by Kleine and other importers—licensed or unlicensed—to market their Italian and French multireel films. An alternative strategy was to sell rights for specific territories to individual entrepreneurs—the "state rights" method, as used years before by Edison in marketing both the phonograph and Vitascope. Often the owner of the film would combine both methods, first exhausting the roadshow potential and then selling off territorial rights so that local entrepreneurs could explore smaller outlets. In this way the film might end its life, worn and abbreviated by repairs, as the special Sunday attraction in neighborhood nickelodeons.

Inevitably the prestige and profit earned by the imported multireel films stimulated domestic feature production. Following the example of the French *film d'art*, producers looking for prestige as well as the assurance of an already proven hit turned to the legitimate stage for both properties and stars. Adolph Zukor had scored a huge success with the French production *Queen Elizabeth*, starring Sarah Bernhardt, which he persuaded the Trust to distribute on a state rights basis. Inspired by this he entered a partnership with Daniel Frohman to produce films of "Famous Players in Famous Plays." The first productions starred James Hackett in *The Prisoner of Zenda* and Mrs. Fiske in *Tess of the D'Urbervilles*. They were followed by Mary Pickford in *The Bishop's Carriage*, James O'Neill in *The Count of Monte Cristo*, Cecilia Loftus in *A Lady of Quality*, and John Barrymore in his first film role, *An American Citizen*. In an interview Zukor promised

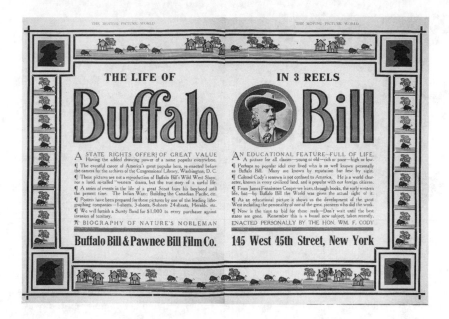

THE LIFE OF   IN 3 REELS

Buffalo Bill

A STATE RIGHTS OFFER{ OF GREAT VALUE
Having the added drawing power of a name popular everywhere.
¶ The essential career of America's great popular hero, re-enacted before the camera for the archives of the Congressional Library, Washington, D. C.
¶ These pictures are not a reproduction of Buffalo Bill's Wild West Show, nor a lurid, so-called "western" drama, but the true story of a useful life.
¶ A series of events in the life of a great Scout from his boyhood until the present time. The Indian Wars; Building the Canadian Pacific, etc.
¶ Posters have been prepared for these pictures by one of the leading lithographing companies—1-sheets, 3-sheets, 8-sheets 24-sheets, Heralds, etc.
¶ We will furnish a Surety Bond for $1,000 to every purchaser against invasion of territory.
A BIOGRAPHY OF NATURE'S NOBLEMAN

AN EDUCATIONAL FEATURE—FULL OF LIFE.
A picture for all classes—young or old—rich or poor—high or low.
¶ Perhaps no popular idol ever lived who is so well known personally as Buffalo Bill. Many are known by reputation but few by sight.
¶ Colonel Cody's renown is not confined to America. He is a world character, known in every civilized land, and is popular with our foreign citizens.
¶ From James Fennimore Cooper we learn, through books, the early western life, but—by Buffalo Bill the World was given the actual sight of it.
¶ As an educational picture it shows us the development of the great West including the personality of one of the great pioneers who did the work.
¶ Now is the time to bid for these reels—Don't wait until the best states are gone. Remember this is a brand new subject, taken recently.
ENACTED PERSONALLY BY THE HON. WM. F. CODY

Buffalo Bill & Pawnee Bill Film Co.   **145 West 45th Street, New York**

■ *The Life of Buffalo Bill*, a three-reel feature, is offered "State Rights"—exclusive distribution rights—for a specific area. Buffalo Bill participated in the film, but an actor portrayed him in scenes from his life.

---

thirty films a year; "We believe that we are doing a sort of missionary work for the higher art—that we are aiding in the cultivation of a taste for better things."

At least one of the licensed companies, Pathé, whose European production gave it a vested interest in features, managed to circumvent the Trust's commitment to the one-reel policy by setting up an unacknowledged arm for the distribution of features, the Eclectic Company. As late as May 1913, however, even Eclectic was advertising that *Les Misérables* "can be shown as a whole or in parts on consecutive days, with special coupon tickets for the course." Paul Spehr suggests that Pathé may not have been alone in having an unacknowledged feature arm. Helen Gardner Feature Plays might, to judge from the number of Vitagraph personnel involved, have been a shadow subsidiary of Vitagraph; and Gene Gauntier Feature Players of Kalem.

The problem for the licensed companies was that the public began to demonstrate unequivocally that it liked feature films and preferred to see them in one sitting. A feature program was a special event. Exhibitors found that their audiences would happily pay twice the normal five cents for a

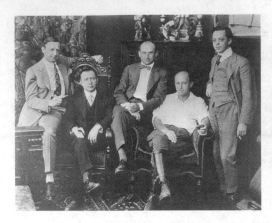

■ Adolph Zukor (seated, second from left), shown with productions partners (left to right) Jesse L. Lasky, Zukor, Samuel Goldfish (later Goldwyn), Cecil B. DeMille, and Al Kaufman in 1915 (above left). Zukor's Famous Players in Famous Plays, an antecedent of Paramount Pictures, produced filmed versions of theater productions. One of the first releases was *The Count of Monte Cristo* (1913), starring the popular stage star James O'Neill in one of his best-known roles (right). O'Neill is remembered today as the father of Eugene O'Neill.

feature presentation without protest. The feature market grew. Between 1912 and 1914 some three hundred were distributed.

Reluctantly the Patents Company acknowledged the multireel film. With Selig's three-reel *The Coming of Columbus* (1912), the most spectacular domestic production to that date, General Film instituted a special feature service, extra to the regular program service. Most of the manufacturers contributed films to this service, although Biograph remained strangely resistant. This was a source of particular discontent to Biograph's star director D. W. Griffith, who found himself in conflict with the company when he insisted he could not do justice to *Enoch Arden* in a single reel (as he had already attempted to do in an earlier version). The film was made in two reels, but inevitably released one reel at a time.

Griffith continued to fight to make features, but as late as 1913 the company shelved his four-reel spectacle, *Judith of Bethulia*, for almost a year, until long after Griffith himself had abandoned Biograph. Biograph's late and poorly calculated entry into features came in June 1913, with an agreement to film the successes of the theatrical impresarios Klaw and Erlanger.

In its origins the economy of the nickelodeon was based on short shows and quick turnover. Programs made up of a variety of short films made possible the continuous performance, at which people could enter and leave at any point. The continuous performance was to persist, never entirely to disappear. The new economy of feature films and consequent longer programs, however, demanded larger theaters, suitably equipped for audiences who would stay there for two hours or more.

The coming of the picture palace was a gradual evolution rather than a sudden revolution. The proliferation of the nickelodeons brought competition, and competition stimulated the creation of more impressive, more attractive, more comfortable theaters that could extend their appeal to the better family trade. As more and more theaters were custom built, they vied with each other to provide facilities like restrooms, waiting rooms, and even nurseries. They were decorated to impress, with the greatest possible proliferation of cut-glass mirrors, marble, mahogany, brass and plasterwork (though not always carpets, which were thought unhygienic). The ubiquitous Decorators Supply Company advertised its services in providing decorations, generally prefabricated, to enhance the ornament within and without the theaters. Said a September 1913 ad in *The Moving Picture World*: "Only through the medium of our class of ornamentation can you hope to have your place rank in beauty and attraction with the best in the country. The time is past when a cheaply fixed up place will pay. You must make a strong effort to get a fine Show Place to make money." Sloping floors for better visibility were a facility that few of the original storefront theaters could offer, but which came to be expected in well-appointed theaters.

Longer films demanded two projectors. Many of the old nickelodeons had managed quite happily with a single projector—there were always song-slides or a singer to fill the break for the reel change. Now the singers, the song-slides, and the vaudeville acts began to be considered passé and vulgar. Musical provision grew more elaborate and sophisticated. A good theater required a proper orchestra pit and an organ.

Already many legitimate theaters had been converted into motion picture houses. By the end of the first decade of the century new purpose-built theaters of comparable size and stature began to appear. Every week the trade press carried reports on these new theaters and the ever-improving facilities they offered to their patrons. Typical is a description from *Moving Picture World* of a $60,000 picture house, with a modest 750 seats, that opened late in 1912 in Zanesville, Ohio:

> The lobby is beautifully lighted and standing in conspicuous places are neatly framed posters of the pictures constituting the day's program.

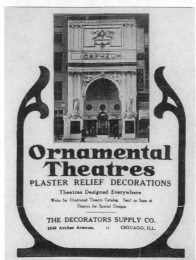

■ Before radio and TV, a small town like Corning, Ohio, could support two theaters (top). Converted stores like the Majestic Theater were gradually replaced by more elegant houses. The Decorators Supply Company sold prefabricated decorations and other items to improve the appearance of theaters and enhance their appeal to a "better class of clientele." This ad appeared in *Moving Picture World*, September 6, 1913 (left). Samuel L. "Roxy" Rothapfel pioneered the development of the movie palace (right). Roxy believed that the experience of being in a theater should be as good or better than the film being shown.

There are check rooms for women's and men's garments, wraps, etc. The checking system of the house is so perfect that a man may have his cigar checked and get it back in good condition when the entertainment is over. The ushers and attendants are examples of refined etiquette and neatness of appearance. As one sits in the luxurious leather opera chairs watching the pictures, he breathes nothing but the purest of air, for the ventilating apparatus of the theater is perfect. It is cool in the summer and the right temperature of warmth permeates the place in winter.

The music was provided by a Wurlitzer unit orchestra and a pipe organ. *Moving Picture World* also noted as a particular mark of the success of the house: "People from neighboring towns come to this house in automobiles."

Early in 1910 Samuel L. ("Roxy") Rothapfel, destined to be known as "the Belasco of motion pictures," began a regular column on showmanship in *The Moving Picture World*. Only two years before, Rothapfel had given up door-to-door selling to open a nickelodeon in the backroom of a saloon in Forest City, Pennsylvania. The flair and showmanship he displayed attracted the notice of the Keith circuit, who consulted him on their vaudeville film presentations. From this he became manager of the Alhambra, Milwaukee. Late in 1913 he arrived in New York, to retrieve the fortunes of the Regent Theatre on the corner of Seventh Avenue and 116th Street, built earlier that year to the designs of Thomas Lamb.

As made over by Rothapfel, the stage of the Regent, said *Motion Picture News*, "represents a conservatory. The musicians play on the stage and are partly hidden by potted plants and other decorations including an electric fountain. Two large windows open on either side of the screen, with appropriate backgrounds, giving a perspective to the scene. Here the changing lights of varied colors procure a most wonderful effect. A heavy velvet curtain is lowered in front of the screen between the pictures, when the singers appear at the windows or the orchestra plays a special selection. It is art in every sense of the word, and there is no wonder that a manager paying so much attention to all the details is rewarded by constantly increasing patronage."

Years later Rothapfel rationalized the function of such splendor: "I want to make the truck driver and his wife feel like a king and queen."

THE YEAR 1913

The cinema comes of age

THERE WAS NO REASON WHY THE YEAR 1913 SHOULD
have a special magic, yet a number of developments in the motion picture
world were coincidentally consolidated to make these twelve months a watershed in the story of American cinema. Looking back from 1913, the two
decades since W. K. L. Dickson registered the first motion picture film for
copyright had been a period of experiment and evolution. Looking forward,
the future structures of the industry were already definitively shaped.

By 1913 the power of the Trust (the Motion Picture Patents Company)
was ebbing fast. In the liberated atmosphere that resulted, new companies
and combines were forming. The migration from East to the wide-open West
was accelerating. The multireel film, still exceptional in 1912, would be quite
normal by 1914. Film content was acquiring new variety and sophistication,
and film production aspired to ever greater opulence. The star system had
become a key factor in marketing films. American production had finally
overtaken that of Europe, whose last year of the old era this was to be: a
world war was to change the geography and the politics and the markets, so
that the European film industry could never again recapture its old
supremacy. The movies were America's national art and Americans' undisputed favorite pastime. The great new picture palaces symbolized the age of
prosperity and splendor upon which the cinema was ready to embark.

Production

STUDIOS

Over the years the original East Coast glass-house studios had been
enlarged and technically improved with the addition of artificial lights and

well-equipped production departments. In 1912 the Selig studio in Chicago was reckoned the largest and most advanced of the eastern establishments:

> It is devoted exclusively to making films, and finds employment for 400 hands. The main studio, in which are two stages, measures 179 feet in length by 80 feet wide. In addition to this indoor establishment, there are between two and three acres of surrounding land which have been enclosed for outdoor work. This field, if such it may be called, presents a strange sight. It is dotted with little groups of scenery. Here is a medieval castle with ruined battlements; a few yards away to the right is a modern street; while on the left is the interior of a stately drawing-room. In one corner are a number of artificial hills fashioned by the dumping of earth, criss-crossed with paths and trails. It is an incongruous medley of periods and scenes, but one and all little assemblages of back-cloths and wings represent a stage, and one and all face the southern sun. Upon these little stages the plays are produced.

The Selig Chicago studio also had an artificial pool of 60,000 gallons, "where a lake, lagoon, or swamp environment can be secured." In New York, the Edison water tank had a capacity of 130,000 gallons.

The new studios built in California by Universal and the New York Motion Picture Company, however, dwarfed these urban installations. They were like small cities, covering acres of inexpensive real estate. The Californian climate, which would generally have made glass roofs intolerable, favored the use of open-air stages, covered with linen diffusers to soften the sunlight.

DIRECTORS

As ambitions expanded, so did the size of the film unit, with increasing specialization of crafts—direction, writing, acting, photography, editing, design. In the early days films were made virtually single-handed by cameramen-directors like Porter and Blackton. By 1913 the director had acquired his definitive role as the dominant figure in the artistic creation of a work produced by group effort.

The second generation of directors tended to come from the theater, like Griffith or Sidney Olcott of Kalem. Olcott, who had begun his career as a stage actor, added to a good sense of story structure a particular penchant for using locations—whether Ireland, Florida, or the Holy Land—to serve the story. At Vitagraph, George D. Baker, originally an illustrator like the company's co-founder J. Stuart Blackton, created the John Bunny comedies, and helped give

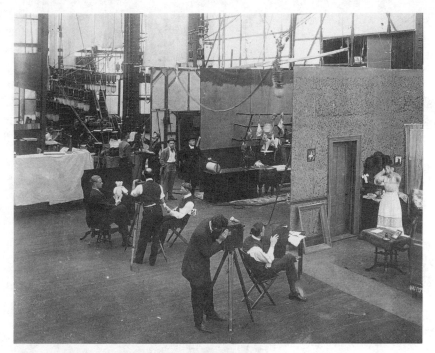

■ In 1907 when Edison moved into this studio in the Bronx, it was the most advanced in the country (left). Glass admitted natural light to the stages and was supplemented by electric lights (above). There were dressing rooms, facilities to design, build, and paint sets, and storage for lighting, costumes and props.

Vitagraph pictures their strong visual sense. Edison's directors after Porter—J. Searle Dawley, Charles Brabin, Ashley Miller—by 1913 still tended to a rather conservative, stagey style. One of the most promising of the new generation was Francis Boggs, engaged by the Selig Polyscope company in 1907, but murdered in 1911 by a studio employee. Alice Guy Blaché, the world's first woman director and founder of Solax, was the advance guard of a group of French directors who were soon to arrive at Eclair and Pathé.

■ A former stage and screen actor, Sidney Olcott directed films for the Kalem Company and his own production company. Olcott often used natural locations to enhance his stories.

WRITERS

The huge production of one-reel films and the new, more complex requirements of multireel features created an insatiable demand for film subjects, and placed a new premium on writers. Through the first decade of the century, studios generally paid five dollars for a story idea, which would then generally be improvised by the director without need for a written script. By 1913 prices for scenarios had risen tenfold and more, and the Italian Cines Company created a sensation when it offered an international prize equivalent to one thousand English pounds for an original idea suitable for a major production. The English magazine *The Kinematograph and Lantern Weekly*, praising Cines for "being courageous enough and honest enough to offer a reward for talent," commented that the parsimony of film companies both with money and with credit had so far been a major inhibition to good film writing.

By 1913 however this was becoming an organized craft. In 1912 the Edison Company began to publish the names of writers—even before consistently crediting the director. Writers now needed the specialist expertise to create scripts that provided workable blueprints for production. Highly technical manuals began to appear—three in 1913 alone. Epes W. Sargent's *Technique of the Photoplay* was based on articles that had appeared in *The Moving Picture World*. J. Berg Esenwein and Arthur Leeds' *Writing the Photoplay* appeared as one of a series of books on literary technique, "The Writer's Library," indicating that writing was now recognized as a legitimate field of literary activity. Eustace Hale Ball, author of *The Art of the Photoplay*, was himself a prominent film writer.

These authors encouraged a very self-conscious discipline for the craft. Esenwein and Leeds exhorted their students:

> Learn, then, to think of a photoplay as being a story in action, instead of in words; a drama in from fifteen to—in exceptional cases—fifty scenes, instead of, as in the spoken play, in three, four, or five acts.
>
> Action is the most important word in the vocabulary of the photo-playwright. To be able to see in fancy his thoughts transformed into action is to have gained the goal for which every photoplay writer strives.
>
> A photoplay, then, as seen on the screen, is a coherent story, with action, gestures, facial expressions, and grouping of the characters, taking the place of dialogue and written description, as in a novel or a short-story . . . the photoplay writer depends upon his ability to *think* and *write* in action.

The manuals advised writers to look for subjects in the newspapers, which ensured a contemporary urgency in subjects, but also helped evade the perils of copyright. In 1907 Kalem had incautiously produced an unauthorized film adaptation of General Lew Wallace's best-seller *Ben Hur, A Tale of the Christ*. It should have known better: eleven years before, the English firm of Riley had made a series of lantern slides of *Ben Hur*, whereupon General Wallace brought suit for breach of copyright against Riley's New York branch. Riley's case was upheld on the general principle that the slides were illustrations rather than a dramatic representation. Kalem could offer no such defense when the Wallace estate brought an action against it, and was obliged to pay damages of $25,000 with costs. Kalem was more fortunate with its adaptation of *The Merry Widow*, made at the same time, which was merely injuncted.

■ Good stories made good movies and good movies made profits. In 1911, writer-lecturer Epes Winthrop Sargent began a series, *Technique of the Photoplay* in *Moving Picture World* (left). The series was published as a book in 1913. Plagiarism was commonplace. In December 1911 he warned that a court's decision in the *Ben Hur* case meant that writers could no longer use copyrighted works as a story source without paying the authors (right).

The *Ben Hur* case however made producers and writers more sensitive. There was a vogue for classics safely out of copyright, but by 1913 film companies were chasing prominent living writers like Jack London and Rex Beach, whose collaboration was widely publicized and legitimately rewarded.

Like other workers in the burgeoning industry, writers were developing a jealous pride in their own importance. In a later manual, *The Photodrama* (1914), Henry Albert Phillips regretted that:

A power has risen in the production of the photoplay . . . that has often hampered the progress of the new drama. All authority, in too many instances, has been given to the director. Even though the meaning of the word classic was as remote from his understanding as the study of astronomy, yet all manuscripts were subject to his interpretation, alteration, and elimination, from "Lucile" to "Lear." Too often actors en masse have had no further intimation of what they were doing than the vociferous bellowings of a director beyond the camera. Thus was the writer deprived of his most necessary ally in the interpretation of his finer dramatic ideas.

This was a battle the writer would never win; even though

> Photoplay writing is bound to become a dignified profession despite the obloquy that seemed to rest upon it for so long. But the photoplaywright must elevate himself thru his artistic product and thru a demand for recognition of meritorious work by appropriate compensation and also by credit of his name to appear on the screen as author of his plays.

One important aspect of the writer's work was the placing and writing of intertitles, or "leaders" as they were still called in 1913. Intertitles had first been introduced to describe the action in the shots, supplying the original role of the "lecturer." Gradually their use had become more subtle and complex. Esenwein and Leeds advised that "Properly used, leaders can accomplish four results very satisfactorily: (a) mark the passage of time; (b) clear up a point of the action which could not otherwise be made to 'register'; (c) 'break' a scene; and (d) prepare the mind of the spectator to enter into the scene in the right spirit."

The same authors described a use of the intertitle still fairly novel in 1913, but which was soon to become dominant practice: to provide the dialogue supposed to be spoken in the shot following the title: "wherever the newer form can be used to advantage it is less objected to by the audience than in the bald statement sub-title—doubtless because it is in line with the illusion of reality in using the players' words, and is not merely an insertion by the producer or the author, as other inserts evidently are."

Progressive critics like W. Stephen Bush in *The Moving Picture World* considered "that the perfect photoplay has no leaders and needs none. Certainly, such a picture would be ideal, since it would be so perfectly acted and so absolutely self-explanatory that no inserted explanations of any kind would be necessary." There were a few attempts to demonstrate this ideal, notably Vitagraph's *Jealousy*, a solo tour-de-force by Florence Turner, in which "the woman's every thought, so to say, was portrayed and understood by the audience as if the play were accompanied by a printed synopsis of the story."

Such experiments were necessarily exceptional, but Bush shrewdly counseled in *The Moving Picture World* (October 4, 1913), "When you find that the need of titles grows less and less as you approach the middle and the end of your story you may be reasonably sure that your feature has in it the promise of success."

ACTORS AND STARS

Griffith, choosing inexperienced but fresh young players instead of stage-inducted veterans, exerted a major influence upon acting styles. There was acute recognition that films demanded their own styles of acting, and the trade press was full of articles on "the silent pantomime." When the European mime artist Pilar Morin appeared in America in the classic mime play *L'Enfant Prodigué* she was feted by the film community and became for a short time a guru of the new acting, although after a few months, having failed to exert the expected magic, she was advertising for work. Her sentiments, as recorded by *The Moving Picture World* were sound enough: the general run of screen actors, she intimated "do not think and feel, and therefore they do not convey their emotions to the audience. If they really thought and felt, as they are supposed to be thinking and feeling, when the photograph is being taken, then our pictures would be full of dramatic action, conviction—the act would 'get over.'"

Although the old, exaggerated ham styles demanded in days of the unvarying long-shot persisted, Madame Morin's principle was by 1913 becoming accepted as the common wisdom. The increasing use of close shots favored and in fact demanded a more subtle, interiorized kind of playing.

The year 1913 saw the star system finally in place. In the first decade of the century, with the rare exception of stars from other fields who made publicized appearances in films, actors remained anonymous. This suited everyone. For respectable stage actors, working in "the galloping tintypes" was the last desperate resort, a clear admission of failure and disgrace. Some theatrical managements absolutely prohibited their artists from working in films.

The film manufacturers for their part were concerned to sell their films as factory products, depending on the public's loyalty to brand names. Apart from the caprices of popularity, actors tended to move from one company to its rivals, so there seemed little encouragement to build up individual star names. Above all was the manufacturers' justified fear that if actors were named and known to the public, they would demand much higher salaries, related to their popularity, like stage and vaudeville stars.

■ Mary Pickford, the screen's first super star, began her film career in 1909, as an unpublicized performer at Biograph. The public knew her only as "Little Mary" until she was hired by Carl Laemmle's IMP Company in 1910. By 1915, her face as well as her name was familiar to fans throughout the world.

The public however unequivocally identified its favorite actors, and wanted stars. In the undated *Motion Picture Making and Exhibiting*, John R. Rathbun noted:

> Many theaters have "special program" nights on which they exhibit one certain make of film only, regardless of the subject. A permanent announcement board at the front of the theater lists the nights on which the admirers of any one producer can view his favorite film: "Selig night, Tuesday"; "Essanay night, Wednesday"; and so forth. The success of this arrangement is due to the popularity of the actors and actresses employed by the different film concerns, whom the moving picture fans regard in the same light as "matinee idols" of the legitimate theater are worshipped.

If the manufacturers would not identify the stars, then the audience would, and so Florence Lawrence became "The Biograph Girl," Florence Turner, "The Vitagraph Girl," and Mary Pickford, "Little Mary." The companies yielded to the inevitable. Kalem, in 1909, seems to have been the first to identify its stock players, and most of the other manufacturers quickly followed suit. On March 12, 1910, Carl Laemmle adopted a sensational stunt to publicize his capture of Florence Lawrence from Biograph. Advertisements headed "We Nail a Lie" purported to deny rumors "that Miss Lawrence (the 'Imp' girl, formerly known as the Biograph girl) had been killed by a street car." Readers were reassured on the contrary that "Miss

■ Before hiring Pickford, Carl Laemmle enticed Florence Lawrence, the "Biograph Girl," to his IMP Company. This ad, which pretends to squelch a rumor (planted by Laemmle himself) that Florence Lawrence was dead, was one of the earliest publicity stunts to promote a star (left). Photographs of stars were distributed to theaters, magazines, and newspapers and sold to eager fans. These are souvenir pictures of Vitagraph's popular comedian Billy Quirk (above left), leading lady Anita Stewart (above right), Kalem's Tom Moore (facing page, left). and Nestor's Dorothy Davenport (facing page, right).

Thomas Moore.
with
Kalem Stock Company

Lawrence was not even in a street-car accident, is in the best of health, will continue to appear in 'Imp' films, and very shortly some of the best work in her career is to be released." Florence Lawrence and Florence Turner were among the stars who pioneered personal appearance tours, always drawing excited crowds.

Biograph alone stood out against the naming of their stars, making it a serious offense for any employee to break the embargo and, it appears, canceling advertising in *The Moving Picture World* after the magazine published Biograph players' names. To satisfy his public, Biograph's British distributor was obliged to invent names to publicize the players: thus to the English Mabel Normand was "Muriel Fortescue," Blanche Sweet "Daphne Wayne," Kate Bruce "Phyllis Forde," Dell Henderson "Arthur Buchanan," and so on. Not until March 1913 did Biograph relent and officially publicize its stars.

Stars now became a key factor in the selling of motion pictures. In October 1913 Laemmle's Universal took a double-page advertisement in *The Moving Picture World* to demand:

> What is the earthly use of showing pictures posed by amateurs and unknowns when you can get the very best known stars of the screen by using that Universal program? . . .The photograph of any star on this wonderful list if displayed in your lobby with the words "Here Today" is positively bound to boost your receipts . . . . Every one of these

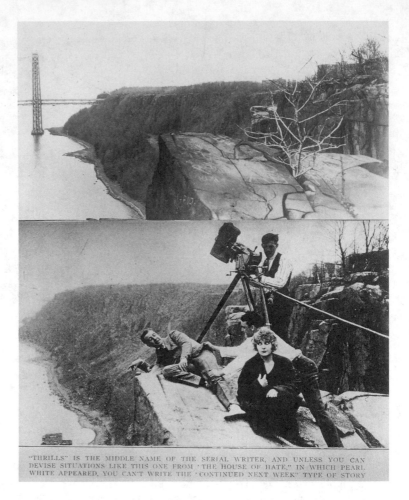

■ Camera operators had to be fearless. Here is Arthur Miller filming fearless Pearl White on the Palisades at Fort Lee, N.J. for a Pathé serial in the days before the skyline changed. The fearless director is George Seitz. Miller won three Oscars for cinematography during a distinguished career.

favorites has a big following. Take advantage of it and *turn their popularity into increased profits for yourself.*

The statement was followed by a list of thirteen male and thirteen female Universal stars, including King Baggot, Warren Kerrigan, Wallace Reid, Florence Lawrence, Marguerite Fischer, Lois Weber, and Pearl White.

■ Developed in England, Kinemacolor was one of several pioneering color processes. It enjoyed a brief success, but it required expensive special projectors that were not compatible with conventional films. Exhibitors who installed the equipment had to rely on the limited supply of films available from the company. This ad appeared in the trade press in 1913.

CAMERAMEN

Seeing films today in prints that have been badly worn and crudely copied during more than three quarters of a century, it is hard to appreciate the achievement of the early photographers, generally working with uncontrollable sunlight and slow and insensitive film stock. Inheriting the great traditions of Victorian photography, there was nothing of the primitive in their work. W. K. L. Dickson, shooting films many months before the Lumières' talented international team, must be reckoned the true father of cinematography. Already an accomplished still photographer, he worked with great variety, using close-up (*The Sneeze*), three-quarter length shots, and exteriors alongside more conventional proscenium set-ups. Dickson's alumni included Arthur White, William Paley and, most notably, G. W. ("Billy") Bitzer, whose virtuoso use of atmospheric lighting is evident in Biograph films even before his historic association with D. W. Griffith. Edwin S. Porter was versatile, resourceful, and also gifted with a strong sense of composition.

Many cameramen who came to prominence in the teens and twenties of the century learned their trade in this formative and fast-developing period, among them Tony Gaudio, Arthur Miller, Henry Cronjager, Dal Clawson, Sol Polito, Phil Rosen, Joseph Ruttenberg, Carl Akeley, Alvin Wyckoff, Hans Koenekamp, Roland Totheroh, Charles Rosher, Arthur Ripley, Carl Louis Gregory, Arthur Edeson. These native artists were reinforced by a flow of fine cameramen from Europe, among them Alfonso Liquori, Alfred Gondolfi, Georges Benoit, Marcel LePicard, and Lucien Andriot.

COLOR

From the beginning of cinematography there were efforts to supply the want of color in the photographic image. The Edison Company had the film

■ Edison finally marketed a sound-and-film system, the Kinetophone, in 1913 (left). It combined a cylinder phonograph with a motion picture projector (below). Synchronization, which worked in controlled demonstrations, sometimes broke down in practical use. As with competing systems, the "morning-glory" amplifier was often inadequate in large theaters.

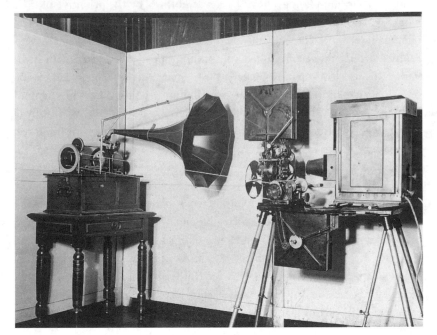

of "Annabelle's Skirt Dance" colored by hand, to imitate the effects produced at live theatrical performances in this genre by projecting limelight through colored filters on to the billowing draperies. In the late 1890s films were short enough to be painstakingly colored by hand, frame by frame, by teams of women workers. The registration was usually very inaccurate, but the flaring colors lent extra excitment to the screen image. In France the Pathé company patented an elaborate and very effective method of applying color by stencils.

Tinting and toning of films remained a widespread practice to the end of the silent period. In tinting, the finished positive print was chemically dyed in a variety of colors; in toning, the silver salts of the film image were chemically colored. Sometimes the two methods were combined to very subtle effect. By 1913 certain conventions were established—blue tints for night scenes, amber for sunlight, red for conflagrations, and so on. The process was elaborate, involving dying each scene of the positive separately and then reassembling the film.

In England, as early as 1899, Edward R. Turner and F. Marshall Lee patented a "natural color" process, that is a system by which color was recorded photographically, and not subsequently applied manually. The Lee–Turner system involved exposing and subsequently projecting successive frames of the film through red, green, and blue filters arranged on a revolving shutter. The process was complicated and never successfully exploited.

The patents, however, were acquired by Charles Urban, an American who had transferred his business to London after patents difficulties with Edison. With his colleague George Albert Smith he developed the principles of the Lee–Turner system to produce the first successful natural color process, Kinemacolor. The basic process consisted in running the film through the camera at double speed, 32 frames a second, with a revolving shutter alternately exposing the individual frames through red and green filters. The positive film was projected through a corresponding arrangement of filters on a similar revolving shutter.

The first successful tests of Kinemacolor were made in 1906, and the process was finally ready for demonstration in 1908. The first public shows took place at the Palace Theater, London, in March 1909. After a triumphant New York premiere at Madison Square Gardens, Urban sold the American patent rights. The Kinemacolor Company of America embarked on an ambitious program of exploitation and production, and endeavored to simplify the technology of the apparatus and bring prices down. By mid-1913, however, the company was sold to the theatrical managers Cohan and Harris, and little more was heard of Kinemacolor.

Gaumont's Chronochrome process, which used three lenses, each with a separate color filter, was introduced in America about the time that Kinemacolor faded out, but never reached the stage of public exhibition. Not until the development of natural color systems, which dispensed with the need for special projection apparatus, did color films become a practical reality.

SOUND

As great stage actors deigned to appear in pictures, whether in the French *films d'art* or in Zukor's Famous Players in Famous Plays, the yearning for sound films became stronger. There had been periodic spates of experiment with talking and singing pictures, and Edison from time to time revived his promise of sound films. Of the various synchronized disc systems, only the Gaumont Chronophone survived for some years, outlasting a flurry of competitors, like Synchroscope, Cameraphone, and Photophone, which coincided with its introduction to the United States in 1908.

All the systems suffered from the handicaps of limited acoustic amplification, and the difficulties of maintaining perfect synchronization. All sorts of mechanical and electrical methods of synchronization were attempted, some involving systems of gears or pulleys connecting the projector at the rear of the theater with the phonograph behind the screen. No system however was proof against a needle jumping a groove or a break in the film.

In March 1913 Edison was finally ready to launch a new Kinetophone, which was advertised modestly as "Talking Pictures. A Fact! A Reality! Thos. A. Edison startles the civilized world and revolutionizes the picture business with his latest and greatest invention THE KINETOPHONE absolutely the first practical talking picture ever made." After the first lukewarm reviews, which suggested that the synchronization was adequate but that the sound quality and volume left something to be desired (the system used cylinder records), the Kinetophone proved a failure. Although the results in controlled demonstration conditions were satisfactory, in theatrical use the synchronization could easily go badly astray. After incidents in which audiences booed the Kinetophone, the Keith-Orpheum circuit paid to terminate its contract with Edison.

MARKETING

With the star system arose a new industry as audiences clamored for souvenirs of their favorites. On both sides of the Atlantic there was a huge trade in picture postcards; and in Europe of cigarette cards portraying the stars along with the insignia of their employer companies. With the star system the fan magazine also came into being. In 1911 J. Stuart Blackton began *Motion Picture Story Magazine* (subsequently *Motion Picture Magazine*) to publicize Trust films and stars. The following year *Photoplay* began its life as a cinema program magazine. Both became influential and long-lasting fan magazines, and inspired innumerable imitators.

The film souvenirs and fan magazines became part of the fast-growing marketing machine. The first professional film publicists were recruited and all the techniques of modern publicity—press shows, press releases, planted gossip stories, and a calculated wooing of the rising breed of film columnists—developed with them. Advertising became more sophisticated. Illustrated posters, exceptional before 1910, were now produced for practically every film, and in great variety for the more important feature productions.

In the wake of the booming trade and booming publicity, trade periodicals—*Views and Film Index*, *Motography*, *The Moving Picture World*, and *Motion Picture News*—flourished and expanded voluminously. In these periodicals were the origins of serious film criticism. Although reports of individual films rarely went beyond annotated synopses, the editorial essays of writers like W. Stephen Bush, Louis Reeves Harrison, Epes Winthrop Sargent and, in the film section of *The New York Dramatic Mirror*, Frank Woods, provided an influential critical commentary on the progress of film art. For this generation of critics were convinced, above all, that film was an art; and their constant exhortation to filmmakers to improve the art and the functions of the cinema are heroic and touching.

Exhibition

THEATERS AND AUDIENCES

Seeing the films and reading the film journals of 1913 the most striking impression is an overall sense of respectability, order, wholesomeness. No

■   The first fan magazines featured prose versions of the movie plots but the format changed because fans kept asking for photographs, gossip, and articles about film personalities. The earliest, *Motion Picture Story Magazine* (later *Motion Picture Magazine*) was published to promote the Trust's films. Thomas Edison was the star who graced the cover of the first issue in February 1911. *Photoplay Magazine* started in 1912. Its July 1912 issue featured a scene from *The Fall of Black Hawk*, American Film Company's drama of Abraham Lincoln's early life (center). Industry trade magazines also flourished. They printed advertising, data about new releases, and information about companies and people working in the industry. The August 17, 1912, issue of *Motography*, published in Chicago, features Eugenie Besserer and Hobart Bosworth in a scene from Selig's 1912 version of *Monte Cristo* (bottom).

■ Clean, comfortable, orderly theaters and concern for the audience were the hallmarks of wholesome family entertainment. Uniformed ushers were a sign of quality. The March 12, 1910, issue of *The Moving Picture World* features ads from several companies for "up to date," nobby and "cheap" uniforms.

doubt there were still disreputable, disorderly, insalubrious fleapits in slum districts, but these places and their public did not attract the attention of the trade press. As the cinema repertoire aspired to adaptations of the world's classics and the more serious subjects made possible by the scope of the feature film, and as the great luminaries of the stage lent their prestige to the cinema, the democratic base of the audience widened more than ever, to bring in the intellectuals, the respectable bourgeoisie, the educators, and the uplifters.

The exhibitors respected their audience and aimed to make theaters worthy of them, providing fare that should be as spotless as were their houses, outside and in.

It goes without saying that the exterior, that is to say, the entrance of a moving picture theater, should be scrupulously clean and kept free of rubbish and paraphernalia which would have a tendency to obstruct the egress of the public [advised *The Moving Picture World* in a series on "The Modern Moving Picture Theater" in 1909]. If possible, a polite and uniformed attendant should always be present to usher people into

No Sex Problems on the Screen

By W. Stephen Bush.

THE mania for airing and discussing sex problems from the housetops by means of megaphones seems to have hit the motion picture. The screen, of all mediums of expression, is far the least suitable for a display of this morbid publicity. It is not a question of whether this film is good and the other film is bad, the question is much broader than that. Does it benefit the good name of the motion picture to discuss these questions on the screen? Is any real good accomplished thereby? Does the undoubted evil outweigh the doubtful good?

There has long been a tendency in our modern life to dwell upon what is abhorrent and to paint not the rainbow but the details of the abattoir. This tendency which cannot be deplored too much crops out in the newspaper, in the magazine, in the pulpit, on the stage and at last even on the screen. Unquestionably the corruption of women is the worst offense against society and is tantamount to a poisoning of the well-springs of our national life. The law, and the men designated to enforce the law, can have no higher and no more imperative duty than to exterminate corrupters of women. Public sentiment is unanimous on this point and needs no prompting from stage or screen. The evil is known sufficiently well. Effective means are being taken by the states and by the nation to extirpate it and no more is needed. It may have been necessary to awaken the public conscience to a realization of the evil, but this work has now been done most thoroughly and the rest may be left to the officials who are responsible for the enforcement of the laws.

The continuous spreading of morbid details cannot be excused with the specious and overworked plea of conveying wholesome lessons.

The teaching of wholesome lessons is all right and is to be encouraged, but when the teaching process is inspired by the sole desire of making money we have every right to question the sincerity of the teachers. They must not complain when they are suspected of taking a far greater interest in their profits than in the wholesome lessons. Their teaching enthusiasm never carries these teachers away into distributing free tickets to the public. It may be true that a moral lesson goes with every ticket, but every ticket has to be paid for on the highly favorable terms of cash in advance. The plain truth is that these films to which the hideous name of "white slave traffic" has been given are intended to stimulate and exploit the morbid interest in the harrowing details of a sickening and revolting aberration of human souls.

The stage and the magazine have suffered in influence and in public esteem through too much exposure and wallowing in intimate descriptions. We would like to see the screen preserved from a similar loss of prestige and hence our protest.

It is, of course, always easy to get a crowd by a morbid appeal. All the best efforts of our civilization have ever been directed toward stifling and restraining the morbid impulses in human nature. Less than a century ago a public execution was regarded as a great public entertainment and a most precious lesson. We have advanced beyond such conceptions and while we still kill people by mandate of the law we no longer make a public spectacle of the killing. We have greater respect for the dignity of man. Our tastes, too, have changed for the better.

Any step backward is to be deplored. Within the last few months the police have repeatedly interfered with displays of morbidness on the stage. It is the earnest hope of all who love the motion picture that the screen will never stand in need of attention from the police.

The agitation against commercializing vice has brought forth a lot of self-appointed reformers who can see nothing but crimes and horrors and who are all too willing to describe them in most lavish detail. Editorial writers, contributors to magazines, a certain kind of ministers and all eminent sociologists are freely voting themselves into the cabinet of the Almighty. They want to make things over and improve on the work of the Creator. While the palmists and poets of old broke forth into rapturous praise of the "ever glorious works" these men and women, with their eugenic theories and their rabid discussion of all sex questions, put on their glasses and critically shake their heads as they contemplate the government of the universe. These people themselves may be harmless enough, but their persistent and one-sided agitation draws all the morbid element in the community after them, even as carrion attracts the crows. The degenerates of both sexes who delight in following the salacious divorce trials and the sensational murder trials come out in full force, delighted with the scent of scandal. The scent is eagerly taken up by the yellow press, at present the most formidable and diabolical enemy of human progress. The most preposterous notions are set afloat to keep the discussion alive and the imagination of the readers is fed with horrible tales of missing women and young girls stupefied by mysterious hypodermic needles, etc. The contagion spreads again and theatrical managers, who are not at all squeamish in their means of filling their show-houses, appeal to the same morbid sentiment by bringing the sex problem upon the stage. The papers are full of letters from disgusted readers voicing their protests. As one of them points out there has more social harm been done "by the breaking down of the barriers of decent reticence in mixed society than was ever done by the supposititious hypodermic needle of the abductor." The ill-devised among the reformers have reformed nothing and have grossly exaggerated the power and the skill of the tempters. The one thing needful now is to check the ravages of these reformers, to suppress their shocking public exhibitions, to put the curb on the tongues of the heedless."

The consequences of all this ill-advised publicity are easily guessed. The moral miasma spreads. Popular imagination, always easily excited, is contaminated and debased. The evil sought to be suppressed by an excess of publicity grows and invades new fields.

Because nothing affects the imagination more powerfully than the picture in motion, we believe that the screen ought to be kept free from all discussion of sex problems under whatever guise presented. The false claim has been made that John D. Rockefeller, Jr., who has financed a crusade against the corrupters of women, is back of these so-called white slave films. Mr. Rockefeller denies this absolutely, and is on record as deploring "this method of exploiting vice as not only injudicious but positively harmful."

He is quoted as saying that "no films have been based on our work with our approval and consent, we have not endorsed any moving picture shows or plays dealing with this subject now produced in this city and the use of my name in any such connection is absolutely unauthorized."

---

the house and to keep order. A uniformed attendant such as Keith & Proctor and other up-to-date managers have is found to have an impressive effect upon the public . . . a courteous uniformed man will inspire confidence, keep order and attract women and children into the house.

The uplift movement had begun as a defense against the cinema's detractors and would-be censors, but by 1913 it seems to have been an end in itself, without ulterior strategies. Week after week the trade papers carried essays on the proper use and propriety of the screen. In an article "No Sex Problems on the Screen," clearly directed against white slave films like *Traffic in Souls*, W. Stephen Bush declared, "The stage and the magazine have suffered in influence and in public esteem through too much exposure and wallowing in intimate descriptions. We would like to see the screen preserved from a similar loss of prestige and hence our protest." Six months earlier, in another typical article, Bush had inveighed against the excess of fire-arms shown in pictures: "The use of firearms in motion pictures . . . is really a nuisance. . . . The effect of such pictures on the minds of the young, especially on the minds of growing boys, is thoroughly bad."

The general film repertoire of 1913 however contained little to offend Bush's sensibilities. Outside the literary adaptations and the permitted release provided by comedy, serious American films tended to high-toned and improving melodrama in a distinctly "Victorian" style which mixed instruction with entertainment. Social and personal happiness revolved around love, marriage, and the family. Marital fidelity and parental respect were rules that could not be broken without disastrous consequences. Wickedness was consistently punished and virtue was rewarded. However moralistic, films were optimistic.

The economically less fortunate part of the audience was reassured by being shown that money does not bring happiness and (in Lewis Jacobs' words) "it is better to be poor and good than rich and wicked." For the endangered there was usually a last-minute rescue, and for the fallen—into drink or other temptation—redemption, even if only of the deathbed variety. The western was an encouraging embodiment of American virtues—individualism, equality of opportunity, honor. Broncho Billy, the ideal of American manhood, the righter of wrongs, was an archetype of the cowboy hero, although Tom Mix, with his riding wizardry and his cunning, looked forward to another more modern breed of hero.

In *Behind the Mask of Innocence*, the historian Kevin Brownlow has demonstrated that a few directors and a few films of this prewar period did attempt to deal seriously with social abuses and social problems—crime and prostitution, labor unrest, racism, poverty, political corruption. Invariably though, the prevailing optimism and the overriding sense of order prevailed, with atonement, reconciliation, and the happy ending as reassurance of social solidarity.

THE SHOW

Along with its campaign for better theaters and finer films, the trade press campaigned constantly for higher standards of showmanship. There were campaigns to eliminate "vulgar" vaudeville from the picture theaters, and even the singers and song-slides were going out of style in the better houses. The incidentals of film presentation were constantly being elaborated by the best showmen. Some sense of the highest aspirations of the day emerges from *The Motion Picture News*' account of Rothapfel's presentation of *The Last Days of Pompeii* as the opening attraction at the Regent, New York.

It seemed as if the setting were a prerequisite to the picture, that to an educated audience the two should, and must hereafter, go together. . . .

Mr. Rothapfel also achieves a theme in his music. There is the same unity throughout the admirable score with which the picture is accompanied. But predominating, woven delicately here and there in the score, is the soft and beautiful song from *Aida*, symbolic of the tender love story of the picture. The curtain rises to an inspiring prelude from the Regent pipe organ, rendered by Mr. Drew, an accomplished organist. Then with a flare from the orchestra, the dark red velvet curtains before the screen are parted to admit the figure of an actor arrayed in Grecian robes. With excellent intonation he announces the opening scene of the picture. Later, just before the Vesuvius scene, he appears again and for an interlude recites the thrilling lines from Bulwer-Lytton's novel which tell of the mob and its frenzied attack upon Arbaces.

At other intervals the monotony of the "silent stage"—there is bound to be some monotony in the long picture, however inspiring it is—was delightfully broken by the voices of trained singers from the windowed recesses above and at each side of the stage. Soft lights were played upon these windows and also upon the fountain, which plays just in front of the orchestra platform.

The frenzied scenes in the doomed city following the eruption of the volcano were made most realistic by the accompaniment from *Lohengrin* and by a chorus of shrill voices back of the screen.

Mechanically as well as artistically, the presentation was flawless throughout. It was, from every standpoint, the best that has been seen in this city.

MUSIC

Music, as this description indicates, played a big part in the best film presentations. The cinema was never truly "silent." The Lumière Cinématographe was quite soon provided with a musical accompaniment on a Gaveau piano, played by M. Emile Maraval, "pianiste-compositeur." When films were a vaudeville turn, the pit orchestra provided appropriate musical support. The most modest nickelodeon would have a piano player, and in the more ambitious houses he or she might be reinforced by a drummer and violinist. The taste applied to the provision of musical accompaniments depended upon the individual performers. Clarence E. Sinn, having for three years conducted a column "Music for the Pictures" in *The Moving Picture World*, summarized the situation in December 1913:

When music was first introduced into the picture theater any old thing would do—a mechanical instrument playing popular junk or a strong-arm player likewise playing popular junk. He was an enterprising

■ Music and musical instruments to accompany movies came in many forms. M. Welte's Organ Orchestrion, a player-organ, could be played automatically or by an organist (above). Before the juke box, Rudolph Wurlitzer had a one-man band, the Wurlitzer Motion Picture Orchestra (left). Realistic sound effects were used to enhance the show. The Kinematophone promised the sounds of sirens, sleigh bells, gunfire, baby cries, and kisses at the press of a key (facing page).

manager who installed music of any kind in his house at that time, and he naturally wanted the world to know it. Hence they "whooped 'er up" until the music could be heard out on the street. Drums were introduced to add to the volume of sound.

Then the popular demand for more suitable picture music made itself felt, and the pianists and drummers began "working up" their pictures, rather crudely in some instances, still a great step forward. The popular taste now demands that the musical accompaniment shall advance as well as the theater and the pictures shown therein. Hence the increasing numbers of orchestras and pipe-organs. Having got them the managers (and musicians also), naturally want the public to know it, so they are giving the aforesaid public the best music in their repertoire—concert music. Nobody seems to care whether it is consistent with the pictured scenes any more than they cared seven or eight years ago when the popular junk was played exclusively. Here and there a few voices are crying in the wilderness, in protest of the standard overture that ends "slap-bang" in the middle of a pathetic scene.

Gradually the public will get used to the novelty of good orchestras and organs in their favorite photoplay theaters, and begin to crave appropriate music. Then they will get it. Some leaders here and there adapt their music to their pictures, and choose numbers in keeping with the show. There are more who do not, if we are to believe what the correspondents tell us. But for all that, it is a great stride forward.

If Sinn was still dispirited by the general musical situation, there were strenuous efforts to improve it, quite apart from his own very intelligent and forthright weekly exhortations and suggestions to musicians. Since 1909 the Edison and Vitagraph companies had been publishing detailed suggestions for suitable music for each film. Early in 1910 Gregg A. Frelinger published a manual of *Motion Picture Piano Music*.

In 1908, the French film *The Assassination of the Duke of Guise* had a specially commissioned and composed score by Camille Saint-Saëns. Although the film seems to have been shown in the United States without this accompaniment, the occasional practice of commissioning special scores for films became more frequent after 1912, when Adolph Zukor engaged the composer Carl Joseph Breil to prepare a special score for *Queen Elizabeth*. The same year the Kalem Company began to issue (at a charge of 15 cents each) special piano scores for its films, composed and compiled with notable sensitivity by Walter C. Simon. For Kleine's presentation of *The Last Days of Pompeii* in 1913, the Chicago composer Palmer Clark wrote a 50-page score, which was sent out to theater musicians ahead of the screening. (This may have been the score used by Rothapfel at the Regent.)

In 1910 the Rudolph Wurlitzer Company had acquired patents in the Hope-Jones unit orchestra. Wurlitzer advertised that in the first six months of 1913 organs had been installed in 267 theaters. "Think of it!" the advertisement proclaimed; "With *one man* you get the effect of a complete and well balanced orchestra—as high as sixty instruments. the right music with every picture—every effect instantly attainable." Alternative one-man musical methods included the Welte Orchestrion, which could be used either manually or as a mechanical player-organ. The Fotoplayer used ordinary piano rolls with a double tracking system so that instant transitions could be made from one piece of music to another. The Fotoplayer also produced a range of sound effects. While such instruments filled the place of orchestras in smaller theaters, in the major establishments they supplemented them.

SOUND EFFECTS

Alongside music, sound effects were widely used, and Lyman Howe's shows were particularly commended for the sophistication of their accompanying sound. Several firms supplied sound effects machines: the Kinematophone, for example, the subject of a 1913 patent application, would produce, at the

■ More sophisticated programs were presented at the larger movie palaces such as New York's Regent Theater, where Samuel Rothapfel was setting a new entertainment standard (above left). The Regent had an orchestra, an organ (foreground), and singers sometimes appeared in the windowed recesses on either side of the screen (above right). Original scores or musical arrangements were prepared for major releases, such as George Colburn's score for George Kleine's release of *Antony and Cleopatra* (right).

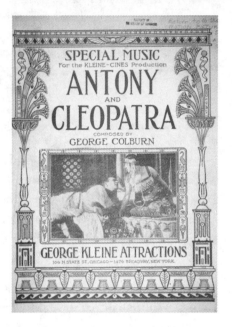

SPECIAL MUSIC
For the KLEINE–CINES Production
ANTONY
AND
CLEOPATRA
COMPOSED BY
GEORGE COLBURN

GEORGE KLEINE ATTRACTIONS
106 N. STATE ST. CHICAGO — 1476 BROADWAY, NEW YORK.

touch of a key, effects ranging from applause, crying babies, marching feet, and a large variety of animal noises to the sound of a kiss. An editorial complaint in *The Moving Picture World* in 1909 indicates how high were critical expectations of sound effects: "In almost all theaters some attempt is made to imitate the hoofbeats of running horses, but the noises are exactly the same whether the horse is running over hard or soft earth. The quick, sharp ring of a hoofbeat on a hard road is quite different from the hoofbeat on a sandy road or on grass ground, yet in practically all theaters they are made the same."

In the twenty years between 1893 and 1913 then, the motion picture and its audiences had ascended from the peepshow to the palace. This short span of time had seen the creation of a great and still growing industry; of the most universal entertainment form in history; and, in the minds of a few, the certainty that this strange hybrid medium had in it the makings of an art.

In an article entitled "Next Year," written on the eve of 1914, Louis Reeves Harrison reflected anxiously:

> What will our descendants think when they come to see how we live? We are very much swelled up at present because a few bright minds in our midst have led us along at what appears to be a lively pace, but what will the people of 2014 think of us when the scrolls of our present life are unrolled for inspection? It would be a joke on us if they sized us up by what has been put on the films of 1913.
>
> Is it not possible for us to preserve in the "canned" dramas of 1914 better representation of what is actually passing in our minds and careers? . . . Would it not be more entertaining to see us as we are in the struggle with inner self and outer influence, strong of intention and weak of performance, than people of other days about whom we know little and care less?
>
> Is there not a rich field of comedy material in the vanity of men who are lucky accidents in the moving picture business, made wealthy before they had time to learn to use their knives and forks, to say nothing of the English language? . . . We need the imagination of genius to enable us to see these things.
>
> There are powerful pictures to be conjured up before our eyes in 1914! Let us read the stories of real men and women on the screen—we are tired of costumed puppets dangling on strings and long for such truth of representation as may engage our hearts and minds.

These were great expectations for a young art of twenty years. Harrison need not have feared: his descendants cannot easily withhold their awe at the aspirations and striving of the film world of 1913.

PRINCIPAL WORKS CONSULTED

Anderson, Robert. "The Motion Picture Patents Company: A Reevaluation." In Balio, ed., *The American Film Industry*.

Balio, Tino, ed. *The American Film Industry*. Madison: University of Wisconsin Press, 1976.

Ball, Eustace Hale. *The Art of the Photoplay*. New York: Veritas, 1913.

Barnes, John. *The Beginning of the Cinema in England*. Newton Abbot, Eng.: David and Charles; New York: Barnes and Noble, 1976.

—*Filming the Boer War*. London: Bishopsgate Press, 1992.

—*Pioneers of the British Film*. Vol. 2: *Jubilee Year 1897*. London: Bishopsgate Press, 1983.

—*The Rise of the Cinema in Great Britain*. London: Bishopsgate Press, 1983.

Bernardini, Aldo. *Ciema muto italiano*. Vols. 1–3. Rome; Barí: Laterza, 1980–82.

Bitzer, Billy. *Billy Bitzer: His Story*. New York: Farrar, Straus, and Giroux, 1973.

Bowser, Eileen. *History of the American Cinema*. Vol 2: *The Transformation of Cinema, 1907–1915*. New York: Scribner's 1990.

Bowser, Eileen, ed. *Biograph Bulletins, 1908–1912*. New York: Octagon Books, 1973.

Brown, Karl. *Adventures with D. W. Griffith*. New York: Farrar, Straus, and Giroux, 1973.

Brownlow, Kevin. *Behind the Mask of Innocence*. New York: Knopf, 1990.

Coe, Brian. *The History of Movie Photography*. London: Ash and Grant, 1981.

Deslandes, Jacques. *Histoire comparée du cinéma*, vol. 1. Tournai: Casterman, 1966.

Deslandes, Jacques and Jacques Richard. *Histoire comparée du cinéma*, vol. 2. Tournai: Casterman, 1968.

Dickson, William Kennedy Laurie. *The Biograph in Battle*. London: T. Fisher Unwin, 1901.

—*History of the Kinetograph, Kinetoscope, and Kinetophonograph.* New York: 1895.

Dickson, William Kennedy Laurie and Antonia Dickson. *The Life and Inventions of Thomas Alva Edison.* New York: Crowell, 1894.

Dyer, Frank Lewis and Thomas Commerford Martin. *Edison: His Life and Inventions.* New York and London: Harpers, 1910.

Eaenwein, J. Berg and Arthur Leeds. *Writing the Photoplay.* Springfield, Mass.: 1913.

Fielding, Raymond, ed. *A Technological History of Motion Pictures and Television.* Berkeley: University of California Press, 1967.

Frazer, John. *Artificially Arranged Scenes: The Films of Georges Méliès.* Boston: Hall, 1979.

Frizot, Michel, ed. *E. J. Marey, 1830–1904: La Photographie du Mouvment.* Paris: Centre Georges Pompidou, 1977.

George, W. Tyacke. *Playing to Pictures.* London: Heron, n.d. (1912).

Griffith, Linda Arvidson. *When the Movies Were Young.* New York: Dutton, 1925.

Haas, Robert Bartlett. *Muybridge: Man in Motion.* Berkeley: University of California Press, 1976.

Hammond, Paul. *Marvellous Méliès.* London: Gordon Fraser Gallery, 1975.

Hampton, Bemjanin. *A History of the Movies.* New York: Covici, Friede, 1931.

Hecht, Hermann. *Pre-Cinema History: An Encyclopaedia and Annotated Bibliography of the Moving Image Before 1896.* London: Bowker Saur, 1993.

Hendricks, Gordon. *Beginnings of the Biograph.* New York: Beginnings of the American Film, 1964.

—*Eadweard Muybridge: The Father of the Motion Picture.* New York: Grossman, 1975.

—*The Edison Motion Picture Myth.* Berkeley: University of California Press, 1961.

—*The Kinetoscope.* New York: Beginnings of the American Film, 1966.

Hepworth, Cecil M. *Animated Photography.* London: Hazell, Watson, and Viney, 1897, 1900.

Hepworth, T. C. *The Book of the Lantern.* London: Wyman, 1889 and subsequent editions.

Hopwood, Henry V. *Living Pictures.* London: The Optican and Phographic Trades Review, 1899.

Jacobs, Lewis. *The Rise of the American Film.* New York: Harcourt, Brace, 1939.

Jenkins, C. Francis. *Animated Pictures.* Washington, D.C.: McQueen, 1898.

—*Picture Ribbons.* Washington, D.C.: McQueen, 1897.

Kircher, Athanasius. *Ars magna Lucis et Umbrae.* 2d ed. Amsterdam: 1671.

Lahue, Kalton C. *Motion Picture Pioneer: The Selig Polyscope Company.* New Brunswick, N.J.: Barnes, 1973.

Liesegang, Franz Paul. *Dates and Sources: A Contribution to the History of the Art of Projection and to Cinematography.* Tr. and ed. by Hermann Hecht. London: Magic Lantern Society of Great Britain, 1986.

Low, Rachel. *The History of the British Film*, vol. 2: *1908–1914*. London: Allen and Unwin, 1949.

Low, Rachel and Roger Manvell. *The History of the British Film*, vol. 1: *1896–1906*. London: Allen and Unwin, 1948.

Merritt, Russell. "Nickelodeon Theaters, 1905–1914." In Balio, ed., *The American Film Industry*.

Mozley, Anita V. *Eadweard Muybridge: The Stanford Years*. Palo Alto: Stanford University Press, 1972.

Muddle, E. J. *Picture Plays and How to Write Them*. London: Cinematograph Press, 1911.

Musser, Charles. *History of the American Cinema*. Vol. 1: *The Emergence of Cinema: The American Screen to 1907*. New York: Scribner's, 1990.

Muybridge, Easweard. *Animals in Motion*. London: Chapman and Hall, 1899.

—*The Human Figure in Motion*. London: Chapman and Hall, 1901.

Niver, Kemp R. *Early Motion Pictures; The Paper Print Collection in the Library of Congress*. Washington, D.C.: Library of Congress, 1985.

Niver, Kemp R., ed. *Biograph Bulletins, 1896–1908*. Los Angeles: Locare Research Group, 1971.

Paerl, Hetty et al. *Ombres et Silhouettes*. Amsterdam/Paris: Chene Hachhette, 1979.

Pathé, Charles. *De Pathé frères à Pathé cinéma*. Lyon: SERDOC, 1970.

Pratt, George, ed. *Spellbound in Darkness*, rev. ed. Greenwich, Conn.: New York Graphic Society, 1966.

Ramsaye, Terry, *A Million and One Nights*. 2 vols. New York: Simon and Schuster, 1926.

Rathbun, John B. *Motion Picture Making and Exhibiting*. London: T. Warner Laurie, n.d. (1914).

Rittaud-Hutinet, Jacques. *Le Cinéma des origines: les frères Lumière et leure opérateure*. Seyssel: Champ Vallon, 1985.

Robertson, Etienne-Gaspard. *Mémoires récréatife, scientifiques, et anecdotiques*. 2 vols. Paris: 1831–33.

Robinson, David. *Lantern Images: Iconographs of the Magic Lantern, 1440–1880*. London: The Magic Lantern Society of Great Britain, 1993.

Sadoul, Georges. *Histoire générale du cinéma*. Vol. 1: *L'Invention du cinéma, 1832–1897;* vol. 2: *Les Pionniers du cinéma, de Méliès à Pathé, 1897–1909*. Paris: Editions Denoel, 1947, 1948.

Sadoul, Georges, ed. *Emile Reynaud, peintre de films*. Paris: Cinémathèque Française, 1946.

Sargent, Epes W. *Technique of the Photoplay*, 2nd ed. New York: Moving Picture World, 1913.

Smith, Albert E. *Two Reels and a Crank*. New York: Doubleday, 1952

Spehr, Paul C. *The Movies Begin: Making Movies in New Jersey, 1887–1920*. Newark, N.J.: Newark Museum, 1977.

Stable, Zdenek. *Queries Concerning the Horice Passion Film*. Prague: Film Institute. 1971.

Microfilm

Musser, Charles, ed. Motion Picture Catalogue by American Producers and Directors, 1894–1908. 6 reels. Frederick, Md.: University Publications of America, 1985.

Memorabilia

Programs, posters, catalogues, and other ephemera in the collections of the Library of Congress, Washington, D.C.; the Edison National Historic Site, West Orange, N.J.; and the author.

Journals

The Biograph. London, issues of 1908–1913.

Edison Kinetograph. London edition, issues of 1910–1913.

1895 Bulletin de l'association française de recherche sur l'histoire du cinéma. Paris: 1986–.

The Moving Picture World. New York, issues of 1907–1913.

La Nature. Paris, issues of 1872–1913.

The New Magic Lantern Journal. London, 1978–

The Optical Magic Lantern Journal, subsequently.

Kinematograph and Lantern Journal, subsequently.

Kinematograph and Lantern Weekly. London, issues of 1889–1913.

Views and Films Index, New York, 1906–1911.

PICTURE CREDITS

Black and White

Frontispiece: "Limbs and Lenses." *National Police Gazette*, November 24, 1894.

INTRODUCTION

Edison Kinetoscopic Records. LC.

CHAPTER 1. PIECES IN A PUZZLE

PICTURE CREDITS

INDEX

note: *Italic* numbers = illustrations.

Geissler tube, 15, 16

Gelatin bromide dry plate, *see* Dry-plate photography

Gene Gauntier Feature Players, 115, 145; *see also* Gauntier, Gene

General Film Co., 104–5, 146; *see also* Motion Picture Patents Co.

General Flimco, 104, *105*

Geneva, Switzerland, 49

Geneva stop movement (maltese cross), 11

Genres, motion picture, 71, 72, 74, 119, 121, 122, 130; *see also specific types under* Chase; Comedy; Melodramas; Spectacles; Trick; Western

Georgia (state), 58, 59

Germany, German, 10, 25, 41, 60, 85, 96, 109, 137, 139

Gilmore, William E., 45, 46, 54, 59, 60, 103

Gish, Dorothy and Lillian, 130

Glasgow, Scotland, 62

Glass plates, 10, 11, 12

Golden Beetle, The (Le Scarabee d'Or) (motion picture), photo insert [*15*]

Goldfish, Samuel (later Goldwyn), 117, *146*

Gondolfi, Alfred, 163

Gossip, 167

Gounod, Charles François, 77

Graham, Evelyn, *118*

Grand Cafe, Paris, 61, photo insert [*6*]

Grand Central Palace, New York City, 86

Grandma's Reading Glass (motion picture), 122

Grant's Tomb, 122, *123*

Great Breach, The (La Grande Breteche) (motion picture), 135

Greater New York Film Rental Co., 95–96, 105

Great Northern Film Co., 104

Great Train Robbery, The (motion picture): Edison's, 1903, 80–82, *81*, 89, 121, 125; Lubin's, 1904, *81*, 82

Greece, Greek, 59

Gregory, Carl Louis, 163

Griffith, David Wark, 116, 125–30, *126*, 139, 142, 146, 163; motion pictures by title, *126–27*, 128, *129–130*, 142, 146

Griffith, Mrs. D. W. (Linda Arvidson), 126, 127, 128

Griffo, Young, 55

Griffo–Barnet fight film (motion picture), 54, 55

Guy, Alice (Alice Guy Blaché), 97–98, *97*, 153

Gyroscope, 31

Hackett, James, 144

Haggar, Walter, 80, 134

Hale, George C., 94–95, photo insert [*14*]

Hale's Tours, 94–95, photo insert [*14*]

Hammerstein's Grand Opera House, New York City, 63–64

Hampton, Benjamin B., 90

Hand-colored motion pictures, 161, photo inserts [*10–11*], [*15*]

Harper's Weekly (periodical), 41, 42

Harriman, Edward Henry, 103

Harrison, Louis Reeves, 167, 176

Harron, Robert, 130

Harvard, Fred, 62

Havana, Cuba, 73

Hazards of Helen (motion picture), 143

Health of audiences, *see* Audiences and spectators

Hearst, William Randolph, 73

Heart of a Race Track Tout, The (motion picture), 115

Held, Anna, 57

Helen Gardner Feature Plays, 145

Henderson, Dell (Arthur Buchanan), 161

Licensed companies, *see* Motion Picture Patents Co.

Licenses and licensees, 90, 101, 102, 104, 105, 107, 109

Life of an American Fireman, The (motion picture), 74, 75, 80

Life of Buffalo Bill, The (motion picture), *145*

Life of Dante, The (motion picture), 136

Life of George Washington (motion picture), 141

Life of Moses (motion picture), 141, 143

Life of Napoleon (motion picture), 141

Light bulb, 54, 69

Lighting and illumination, 3–5, 37; in motion pictures, 24, 31, 33–34, 39, 40, 65, 114, 115, 123, 128, 135, 151–52, 153, 163; in theaters, 149, 161, 171; *see also* Sunlight

Lincoln, Abraham, *167*

Lincoln, William F., 9

Liquori, Alfonso, 163

Lissa, Prussia (Leszno), 16

Litigation, *see* Legal actions, suits, etc.

Little Mary, *see* Pickford, Mary

Liverpool, England, 62

Locations, motion picture, 60, 65, 70, 73, 75, 76, 81, 82, *83*, *84*, 85, 86, 97, 113–119, *116*, *118*, 123, 127, 139, 142, 152, 154, *164*

Locomotion, animal, 12–16, *13*, *14*, *15*, 22

Loew, Marcus, 96

Loftus, Cecilia, 144

Lohengrin (opera), 171

Lombard, Thomas, 37

Londe, Albert, 16, 49

London, Jack, 156

London, England, 4, 6, 7, 22, 40, 47–48, 49, 50, 59–60, 61–62, 71, 95, 96, 134, 139, 165, photo insert [*14*]

Lonely Villa (motion picture), *127*, 130

Long, Samuel, 97, *103*

Los Angeles, Calif., 115, 116, 117; *see also* California

Louis XIV (caricature), 7

Lubin, Siegmund, 71, 87, 96, 101, 113, 115, 125; motion pictures by title, *81*, *82*, *86*, 109, *123*; reenactments, pirating, and plagiarism, 73, 82–83, 122, 123

Lumière, Antoine, 60, 61

Lumière brothers, Louis and Auguste, ix, xi, xii, 60–61, *61*; *see also* Cinématographe

Lumière Co., 30, 85, 101, 104, 133, 163, 171, photo insert [*6*]

Lynching at Cripple Creek, A (motion picture), 125

Lyons, France, 60, 61

M. Welte & Sons, Inc. *172*, 174

McAllister, T. H., 24, 71, 87

McClellan, George B., 107, 109

McCoy, Al, 102

McCutcheon, Wallace, *84*, 85, 125

"Machine Camera Taking Ten Photographs a Second, A" (article), 28

McKinley, William, 64, 80

Macy's department store, photo insert [7]

Madison (James) Council, Library of Congress, ix

Madison Square Garden, New York City, 165

Magazines, 73, 160, 167, 169

Magic Box, The (motion picture), xi–xii

Magicians, 74, 78

Magic Lantern, The (motion picture), *78*

Magic lanterns, *see* Catalogues, lantern slide; Lanterns, lantern shows, and exhibitions

Magnifying glass, 122

Morals, influenced by motion pictures, 84, 106–10, *108*, 134–35, 170; *see also* Censors and censorship; Uplift movement and respectability

Morin, Pilar, 158

Morse, Salmi, 86

Moses, 141

Motion Picture Distributing and Sales Co., 105

Motion Picture Magazine (periodical), 167

Motion Picture Making and Exhibiting (publication), 159

Motion Picture News (periodical), 149, 167, 170–71

Motion Picture Patents Co., 83–84, 101–10, *103*, 113–15, 151, 167; aggressive enforcement of regulations, 102, 113; censorship and uplift, 106–10; legal actions, suits, etc. 105–6, *105*; opposition, 103, 104–6, *105*; standardized production and distribution system, 102, 136, 141–46; *see also* General Film Co.

Motion Picture Piano Music (manual), 174

Motion pictures: *for area of particular interest, see under headings such as* Audiences and spectators; Cameras; Color; Contents and subjects; Distribution; Exchanges; Exhibition; Exhibitors; Film; Genres; Laboratories; Production; Programming; Projection; Studios; Theaters

Motion pictures and lantern slides shows, 70–71, *72*, 80–81, 85–86, 91, 121, 122, 147

Motion pictures as art, 119, 127, 130, 145, 149, 151, 167, 175, 176

Motion Picture Story Magazine (periodical), 167, *167*

Motography (periodical), 167, *167*

Mottershaw, 80

Moving Picture Cowboy, The (motion picture), photo insert [*16*]

Moving pictures, *see* Motion pictures

Moving Picture World, The (periodical), 71, 81, 87, *91*, 92, 94, 96, 102–4, *103*, 106–7, *108*, 109, 134–36, 139, 141, 147, 148, 149, 155, *156*, 157–58, 161, 167, *168*, *169*, 172–73, 175

Multireel motion pictures, 106, 141–44, 151, 154; *see also*: Feature motion pictures; Production of motion pictures

Municipal authorities, *see* Authorities, local, municipal, and state

Musée Grevin, photo insert [*4*]

Music and musicians, 69, 85, 90, 147, 149, 170–74, *175*; accompaniment for motion pictures, 92, 136, 143, 171–74; scores composed for motion pictures, 174; *see also* Opera; Orchestras; Pianos and pianists; Singers

"Music for the Pictures" (column), 171

Musketeers of Pig Alley, The (motion picture), 130

Musschenbroek, Pieter van, 6–7

Mutograph camera, *see* Biograph (camera)

Mutoscope, 50, 55–59, *56*, *57*, 70, 78

Mutual Film Corp., 106

Muybridge, Eadweard, 13–16, *13*, 22, 23, 24, 49

Napoleon Bonaparte, 70, 141

Narratives and mime plays, 6, 7, 12, 80, photo insert [*4*]; *see also* Pantomime; Story films

National Board of Censorship, 109

National Federation of Women's Clubs, 32

National Independent Moving Picture Alliance, 104

Opera, 24, 25, 29, 51, 141

Ophuls, Max, 95

Optical Magic Lantern Journal, The (periodical), 3, 63, 71; *see also Kinematograph and Lantern Weekly, The*

Orange, N.J., 26, 40, 54, 113; *see also* West Orange; Edison, Thomas A.

Orange Chronicle, The (newspaper), 50

Orchestras, 147, 149, 171, 173, 175

Orchestrion organ, *172*, 174

Ore milling (Edison project), *20*, 22, 28

Organs (musical instrument), 136, 147, 149, 171, *172*, 173–174, 175; *see also* Player organs

Othello (motion picture), 136

Ott, Fred, 41, *42–43*

Owen, Ben, *116*

Pacific Ocean, 115

Padua, Italy, 3

Palaces, motion picture, see Picture palaces; Theaters, motion picture

Palace Theater, London, 64, 165

Palestine, 86, 97, 115, 152

Paley, William F., 73, 163

Palisades, N.J., *162*

Palo Alto, Calif., 13

Panoptikon projector, 55; *see also* Eidoloscope

Panorama of the War (film-slide presentation), 80

Panoramas and panoramic views, 94–95, photo insert [*14*]

Pantomime, 12, 93, 125, 130, 158, photo insert [*4*]

Pantomimes Lumineuses (poster), photo insert [*4*]

Paper-base photographic film, 16, 23, 30

Parades, 71, 74

Paramount Pictures, 146

Paris, John Ayrton, 8

Paris, 5, 6, 15–16, 27, 48–49, 61, 73–74, 95, 96, 98, 134, photo inserts [*4*], [*6*]

Paris Exposition, 1900, 73, 95

Passion plays, 82, 85–87, *86*, 144

Pastrone, Giovanni, 136

Patent Office, 23, 25, 29, 39

Patents and patent applications, 10, 11, 12, 16, 19, 34, 38, *39*, 48, 50, 54, 55, *56*, 59, 60, 61, 62, 133, 165, 174; infringement claims and litigation, 27, 33, 96, 101–2, 106, 122–23

Patent wars, *see* Patents and patent applications

Pathé, Theo, 134

Pathé Frères, 87, 101, 103, 122, 134, 135, 144, 145, 153, 165; *see also*: Eclectic Film Co.; motion pictures by title, 124, 134, 135, 137, 145, photo inserts [*12*], [*15*]; U.S. production branch, 97, 113, 142, *143*, 165

Paul, Robert, 50, 59 60, 61, 62; motion pictures by title, 63, 133, 134

Paul, Vincent, 62

Pawnee Bill's Far East Show, 144; *see also* Buffalo Bill & Pawnee Bill Film Co.

Peep shows and peep show devices, 19, 39, 43, 46, 49–50, 51, 53, 55, 56, 58, 70, 176; *see also* Kinetophone; Kinetoscope; Mutoscope; Phantoscope

Pennsylvania, 108, 149; *see also* Philadelphia; Pittsburgh

Pennsylvania Railroad, 83

Penny arcades, *see* Arcades, amusement

People's Institute of New York City, 109

Pepys, Samuel, 4

Perils of Pauline, The (motion picture), 142, *143*

Persistence of vision, xii, 7–12, 34; apparatus, 8–12, *9*, *10*, *11*, photo insert [*2*]

Science fiction, 29; *see also* Verne, Jules

Scientific American, The (periodical),
22–23, 28

Scores, musical, 174, *175*

Scorsese, Martin, xi–xii

Scotland, Scottish, 21, 62

Scott, Sir Walter, 108

Screens, projection, 12, 21, 27, 53, 60,
63, 141, 149

Scripts and scriptwriters, 86, 97, 116,
135, 154, 155; *see also* Writing for
motion pictures

Search for Evidence, A (motion picture),
124, *124*

Seitz, George, 162, *162*

Selig, William, 103, 115–16

Selig Polyscope Co., 96, 101, 113,
115–16, 152, 153, 159; motion pictures
by title, 115, *117*, 125, *142*, 143, 146,
167, photo insert [*16*]

Sennett, Mack, 116

Serials, motion picture, 137, *138*, 142,
142, *143*

Serpentine Dance (motion picture), *44*

Seven Chances (motion picture), 122

Sewing machine, 61

Shakespeare, William, 108, 130, 141

Sheffield, England, 62

Sheffield Photo Co., 134

Sherman Antitrust Act, 105, 106; *see also*
Monopolistic business practices

Ships, 71, 73, 74, 142

Shots, motion picture, 42, 122–28,
129–30, 157; camera position, close-
ups, long-shots, etc., 81–82, 122, 158;
composition and framing, 128–30;
multishot motion pictures, 74–82,
123–124; relationship between, 80,
81, 122, 127, 129–30; *see also*
Cameras, motion picture;
Cameramen; Cinematography
techniques; Scenes

Showmen, 64–66, 70, 71, 85, 89, 93, 121;
see also: Exhibitors

Shutters (projectors and persistence of
vision), 10, *10*, 11, *31*, 33, 34, 54–55,
165; *see also* Intermittent
illumination; Intermittent movement;
Slots

Silent cinema, 171

Simon, Walter C., 174

Sims bill, 84

Singers, 69, 91, 147, 149, 170, 171, 175,
photo insert [*7*]

Sing Loo Chinese laundry, 115

Sinn, Clarence E., 171, 173–74

Slapstick, *see* Comedy motion pictures

Sleeping Beauty (motion picture), 134

Slots or slits (projectors and persistence
of vision), 8, 9, *9*, 10, *10*, 11, 34,
photo insert [*3*]

Smith, Albert E., *103*

Smith, George Albert, 80, 122, 165

Sneeze, The (motion picture), 41, 42–43,
163

Social order, social problems, and social
workers, 108, 124, 125, 130, 169–70

Solax Co., 97, 113, 153

Soldiers, *see* Military

Song of the Shirt, The (motion picture),
127, 130

Songslides, 147, 170; *see also* Lanterns,
lantern shows and exhibitions

Sound, with motion pictures, 21–23, 25,
27–28, 41, 42, 50–51, *51*, 164–65, *164*,
164, 166; *see also* Synchronization of
sound

Sound Beach, Conn., 127

Sound effects, with motion pictures,
136, 172, *173*, 174–175

Sound waves, recorded
photographically, 23

South Africa, 73

South Before the War, The (play), 44